The Unveiling:

A Place Where Pain & Passion Collide

Exposing Trauma & Embracing Love
Julie D. Harper

Scripture quotations marked (NIV) are taken from the Holy Bible, New International Version®, NIV®. Copyright © 1973, 1978, 1984, 2011 by Biblica, Inc.® Used by permission of Zondervan. All rights reserved worldwide. www.zondervan.com The "NIV" and "New International Version" are trademarks registered in the United States Patent and Trademark Office by Biblica, Inc.®

Scripture quotations marked TPT are from The Passion Translation®. Copyright © 2017, 2018, 2020 by Passion & Fire Ministries, Inc. Used by permission. All rights reserved. ThePassionTranslation.com.

Scripture quotations marked (NLT) are taken from the Holy Bible, New Living Translation, copyright ©1996, 2004, 2015 by Tyndale House Foundation. Used by permission of Tyndale House Publishers, Carol Stream, Illinois 60188. All rights reserved.

Cover photograph's © Kelly Stark Photography

Hair color by Amy Vrabel

Hair styling by Sherri Bray

Makeup by Rashin Eskandari

Copy editor / proofreader: Ilana Thomas

Creative advice: Brandon Jones & Amber Royer

This book looks at trauma and recovery from the viewpoint of personal stories. The information presented in this book is meant to be used for general resource purposes only. None of the content of this book should be viewed as medical advice. Specific mental health medical advice should only be received from a licensed professional in that area of study. If you have or believe you have any type of medical or mental issue, you should seek advice from a health care professional for possible treatment options.

Print ISBN: 978-1-66782-641-7
eBook ISBN: 978-1-66782-642-4

To my daughter Sofia…
Your outer beauty is only surpassed by your inner beauty. You have such a sweet, kind, nurturing soul that leaves a path of laughter and love wherever you go.

To my daughter Lily…
Your tenacity and resilience inspire me daily. Your example of strength will open doors for others to follow.

To David Applebaum…
Thank you for being a friend when I needed one. I am forever grateful. "It is what it is."

To Covenant Church, Colleyville, Ricky and Cyd Texada…
Thanks for giving me a church to call home.

Contents

Introduction

<u>Unveiled</u> means to expose something, remove a protective covering or make something public.

Hi, I'm Julie! We don't know each other yet. Or do we? We might find that we are connected in similar ways. Maybe we have experienced some of the same crossroads in life. Or maybe we have not. That is not the point. I believe we all have something to share. The experiences we have each gone through might be the very thing that shines light into another person's darkness. Let me tell you some things about me, and maybe, just maybe, we might have something in common. Throughout my lifetime, I have experienced all the following issues at one time or another:

Neglect

Abandonment Issues

Judgment

Sexual Abuse

Abortion

Depression

Self-hate

Suicidal Thoughts

Anxiety

Promiscuity

Alcohol Abuse

Anger

Hurt

Physical Abuse

Held Hostage At Gunpoint

Became An Introvert

Fertility Issues

In-vitro Fertilization

C-Section

1 Child Born Handicap

Sexually Transmitted Disease

Adoption

1 Child Having Severe Emotional Issues

Financial Hardship

Bitterness

Severe Sadness

Feeling Completely Alone In The World

Betrayal

Divorce

Loss Of Friendships

Feeling Like I Was Losing My Mind

EMDR (Trauma) Therapy

Single Parenting

Dating Again

↓

↓

↓

LIFE!!!

Now, what transpired between this long list of things that I have gone through to feeling untangled and alive again consisted of three things: God, therapy, and forgiveness. Not everyone will have the same story as mine. Each one of us is a unique individual. Our timelines of experiences are distinctive to the person we were created to be. I can tell you, without hesitation, that throughout my life, I feel as though certain revelations have been unveiled to me. Once this unveiling took place, I was able to see specific personal accounts of incidents that impacted me in a whole new light. Then God, therapy, and forgiveness eventually tied everything together. So much so that now when I look back on my life, some of the hardest things I went through were blessings in disguise. Some were building character in me. Some might have happened just so I could help someone else get through the same heartache. Some things I will never understand this side of heaven. But that's okay. Really? Yes, because I would not change a single day of my life. What? You heard me.

More than once I have had people ask me if I could go back and change one day of my life, would I? My answer is always the same, "Absolutely not." Seriously, after all the hard things I just mentioned that I had experienced? Correct. If I changed one day of my life, I would not have the two most precious little humans that call me "Mom," and I would not trade them for the world. Sure, I might have children, but they would not be my two little sweethearts, Sofia and Lily-Grace. I adore being a mom. I consider it an honor that God would allow me to raise these girls and do life with them. Another reason I would not change one day of my life is that every single day, every single thing that has happened, every breath, every tear, has made me who I am today, and I would not trade that for the world either. And trust me, I do not say that with any trace of arrogance or ego. It has taken me 50 years to like me—no, to love me. And my life is beautiful and blessed, so why would I change what has brought me to where I am?

If you would do me the honor of spending some time together here, I would love to go on a journey with you that might possibly be life-changing for you as well. I love happy endings, and I believe, better yet, I know that happy endings are completely possible, even in the midst of a storm in life. As you see, I have been through much. Who hasn't? But I can tell you today, at 52 years of age, I am happier than I have ever been in life. But there were things that had to change within me in order for me to get from where I was to where I am now. Not every step was easy. Most weren't. I truly did not understand everything along the way. There were days I wanted to just give up. And there were days I could not even cry because I was so empty. But none of that is important because the beauty of today erases the ugly of the past, if you let it. I am not going to sit here and say every day of my life is butterflies and roses because we all face struggles, but life really can become beauty from ashes.

When I decided to write this book, I honestly did not know where to begin. As I started jotting down notes and ideas, I decided I would write this book first for my two girls, Sofia and Lily, because if I write it for them, it will keep me honest. They are currently still young, 15 and 10 years old, and there is so much they do not know about their mom's past because all they see is the person I am today. I also wanted to write this for Sofia and Lily in hopes that they would learn from my mistakes and not walk some of the roads that I did. I want them, as well, to realize that mistakes, emotional damage, and so much more can be overcome. Secondly, though, I write this book for the person who has experienced any of the things I have gone through or something completely different. All of us experience challenges, uncertainties, loss, pain. No one is free from adversity in life. But we do not have to let the struggles have us or define who we are.

I feel like I need to paint a picture for you that will somewhat explain the title of the book and give insight into where we are going. I do not believe that there is any such thing as an inopportune moment, at least not with God and the way He talks to me. Let me be totally honest; I was taking a shower when God popped this idea into my head. It was February 23, 2021, on a Tuesday evening. I was not even thinking about this book at the time. I was washing shampoo out of my hair. Then suddenly, God dropped some specific thoughts about the introduction to this book and the first chapter into my sudsy head. Sometimes we have to be in a still, quiet place of peace, warm water running down, steam rising up and just washing the day away, relaxed, in order to hear God speak. And that is exactly how it was that night.

So, let me share with you something that I hope will shine some light and make you think.

When I think about my life, I can unequivocally say that much of my healing had to do with finding truth. Truth that had always been there but had been concealed from me. On the occasion I have some free time to watch television, I must admit that I enjoy shows that have to do with the legal system. Whether I am immersed in a show centered around police or the courts, I am quite fascinated with how truth is found. I get caught up in all the details and how the story unravels. I realize these are merely television shows but there is a reason, I believe, these shows are so popular. And for me, it raises the question, what is it in us the seeks the truth? Is it our hearts? Is it our minds? Or is it all about justice?

Many times, possibly, truth fails to be respectfully represented in our lives. Just as in a court case where lawyers meticulously present strong, well-orchestrated arguments for their clients, but in the end, there is only one truth. There are times that we hear stories of an inmate being released from prison after years of incarceration because new evidence had been procured that exonerated the person accused. It is at that moment that we realize truth was not fully represented previously.

As humans, something arises in us that compels us to search out truth. Some might say that it is our hearts that seek truth. It is our hearts that normally drive our actions. Others might insist that it is our minds that forge for truth. Our minds hold a complex framework full of questions seeking resolve. Then there's justice. Justice evokes something in us that needs closure. Justice gives certitude to a "wrong" done to us in life.

Whether it is our hearts, our minds, or justice that seeks truth, one thing is certain…truth can have a shadow cast upon it when it is seen through human eyes. Eyes that are sometimes tainted by trauma, pain, abuse, indifference and all sorts of other things. I realize I switched gears here but there is a reason for it. Please stay with me.

I personally feel that I found truth with my heart. Our hearts are complex and beautiful. It is our hearts that can be touched in such ways to inspire change. Our hearts are what open us up to the world around us. If you have ever been in love before, you know what it feels like when that special someone enters the room, and you can't help but smile. Or you hear that person's voice, and you feel all warm inside. And when that person holds you, the world stops for a moment. My heart is where my story begins. And I cannot say my heart is also where my story ends because my story is still being written. And so is yours.

So much of our lives are based on perspective. Perspective is the ability, wisdom, and knowledge to comprehend what is important and what isn't. Traumatic events that we have experienced in life can make us believe many untruths about ourselves. Trauma can cloud our perspective and even veil the truth. Truth is a cornerstone and I believe there are people out there in the world that need to unveil the truth that is already there. Court in session…

What truth needs to be unveiled in your life? In my own life, truth was revealed where pain and passion collided. My pain was my complete and total brokenness at all that life had thrown at me. But when my pain collided with God's passion for me, truth was revealed, and healing began. Now, remember I was honest and said that there are some things that I will never understand this side of heaven, but when I totally gave up, gave in, and surrendered my pain, God's passion and love for me brought me to a crossroads in life.

My prayer for you as you read through this book is that your eyes will be opened in some way, you start asking yourself the right questions (because there truly is an enemy that wants to destroy you), you open up to possibilities, you seek help if you need it, and that your life is on a collision course where God will meet you in your brokenness and His passion for you will breathe life back into your wounded places. I have learned so much about God's love for me as He has unveiled things by His love, things that only He could do. Let the journey begin. Love and hugs to you.

Chapter 1

Going Back
Moving Forward

"But there is no Plan B for our life. God only has a Plan A. The Bible says the gifts and the calling of God is irrevocable. I think you can get your license taken away, you can get your Visa taken away, but you cannot get the call of God taken away from your life. No matter how good or bad the past is, the best is yet to come."

--Chad Veach, Pastor and Founder of Zoe Church in Los Angeles, California

You are either about to laugh or roll your eyes at me. I hope I hear the laughter across the miles. "Going Back" has no deep meaning at this exact point and time other than to say if you decided to skip the "Introduction" to this book, I am asking you to be "going back" to read it. The "Introduction" gives some important information about where I want us to go together in the pages of this book. So, please go back and read it. Pretty please? With sugar on top?

Also, I want to make the disclaimer right up front that I am a big fan of quotes, music, and such things that inspire and affirm me and put a smile on my face and determination in my spirit. So yes, I will be including such things throughout this book. As mentioned in my bio for this book, I have worked in television for over 25 years. I am currently a producer for an international talk show in which I have been employed for the past 21 years. Throughout these years, I have had the honor of meeting numerous amazing actors, authors, pastors, businesspeople, missionaries, recording artists, speakers, politicians as well as everyday people that had a story to tell. Many of these people have had a positive influence on my life, and at times I will share some things I learned from them.

An additional disclaimer that I would like to decree is that we are going to be talking about some serious subjects. I am a very "raw" and honest person. I will keep things as focused as I can, and I hope my story, in some way, helps you to find peace, hope, healing and encouragement, as well as forgiveness towards yourself or towards others or both. When I was creating an outline and writing notes before I began this book, God had me go back and read my journals from the last several years. I will be totally honest. I always thought journaling was a waste of time. What? I know, right? But I felt led to start journaling and have continued to do so for years now. Going back and reading through some of what I had written was hard, but some of it brought a smile to my face as I got to see how far I had come. I have gone through some hard stuff. You have gone through, or may currently be going through, some hard stuff. But that's just it; you are going through it. Don't get stuck in it. I was stuck for a long time, and it took me just being sick and tired of me to want to get better. And once I got progressively emotionally healthier, I felt like God told me, "Don't let your pain be wasted. Use it to inspire others."

"You can't go back and change the beginning, but you can start where you are and change the ending."

-C.S.Lewis, British Writer and Lay Theologian

I want my ending to be, "Well done, good and faithful servant." I want to use everything within me to bring positive change wherever and to whomever I can. If the passion in my heart collides with the pain in yours,

I believe God will be in the midst, and change is more than possible. Just as my pain collided with the passion of Christ and He unveiled truth to me that changed my life. So much so that when I was getting ready to start this book, a thought popped into my head about a question to ask my kids. At the moment, I didn't know why I needed to ask this question to Sofia and Lily, but then God expressed to me why this was.

As I mentioned, we will be discussing some serious subjects. Subjects that I now know resulted as trauma in my life. I truly have experienced every single heartache that I mentioned in the "Introduction" of this book. The best word to describe the person I was would be "broken." But as my friend Sheila Walsh says, *"It's amazing what God can do with a broken vessel if you just give Him all the pieces."* I finally gave Him all the pieces. And I went from a broken, bitter, angry, depressed person to someone totally new.

The question I asked my girls was simple. I told them they could be totally honest, say whatever they thought to be true, and they would not get in any kind of trouble. I asked each of them at different times, "What five words would you use to describe mama?"

Sofia, my 15-year-old, actually used seven words:

Organized

Motivated

Caring

Weird (that just means "unique" to me)

Optimistic

Smart

Creative

Funny

Later I asked Lily. At the time, she was 9 years old; she just had her birthday. And she used these words to describe me:

Funny (YAY! 2 times for funny)

Kind

Athletic

Positive

Outgoing

And no, I did not pay them to say those things. But this little experiment of sorts brought some tears to my eyes. Why? Because it validates how far I have come in life, how much healing I have experienced, and it is evidence of what God can do with your life if you open up and give Him all the pieces.

"The only pain God cannot heal is the one you won't release to Him."

-Kim Meeder, Author and Co-Founder of Crystal Peaks Youth Ranch

Trauma is real. Anxiety is real. Depression is real. There may be events that have taken place in your life that you did not even realize could be labeled as trauma. After a couple of years of therapy, I can now look back on my life and cognitively perceive how the actions and words of others negatively impacted my life. My eyes were opened to why I did things the way I did, why I responded to things the way I did, and how to re-train my thought processes and live a better life…a beautiful, happy life at that.

One last thing before we dive into the book. This is just a little FYI about me. My favorite movie of all time is "Steele Magnolias." I seriously have no idea how many times I have watched that positively amazing movie. I could go watch it right now, then watch it again tomorrow. It makes me laugh. It makes me cry. It makes me think. And it makes me laugh some more. Sofia and Lily have never seen it, but oh, it's happening soon. Maybe I should not acknowledge this little family fact, but the most quoted movie in my household is "Nacho Libre." It just makes us all laugh, which shows the maturity level of my family, and we are fine with that. On the other hand, another one of my favorite movies is "The Greatest Showman." Sofia and Lily especially love the songs from the movie, and so do I. We listen to the soundtrack in the car at times, and we all sing along. But one song, in particular, really struck me when I first saw the movie, and it is by far my favorite song. It is the song "This Is Me" written by Justin Paul and Benj Pasek as sung by Keala Settle and The Greatest Showman Ensemble. This song just makes me think of my life, where I have been, what's been done to me, how people treated me in some instances, but then it also reminds me that my life, everything I have gone through, is me. Not only is it me, but guess what? I am still standing. I am happy. I am healthy. I have a beautiful, blessed life. I have the two most amazing children. My life went from broken to beautiful. If you have not heard the song, I encourage you to go on YouTube and listen to it. Due to copyright laws, I cannot include the lyrics, but the song is all about being broken, bruised, full of scars but also brave, bold, and proud of who you are. What's not to like about that? That kind of attitude will make anyone want to get up and dance around the room a little bit. The song is all about empowerment. And your perspective of your life is one of your greatest powers.

"For as he thinks within himself, so is he…"

-Proverbs 23:7 (TPT)

Some of the issues I will be discussing are deep and personal. One or two things I thought about leaving out. Why? Because it is going to completely expose me. But that's okay. If it helps someone reading this, then it is totally worth it. I have faith in God to walk through this with me, just as I have faith in God to walk with you in whatever you need to walk through. As I just mentioned, I will be sharing some deep and personal stories about my life with you. I would like you to have the foreknowledge that these stories of my life obviously include other individuals. It is important that you know I have the blessing of my ex-husband David to share some deep struggles we went through. If we expose hardships that we experienced and overcame, and it can help even one person, then the story is worth sharing. There are other people that are aware of what I have written as well. My mom, my daughter Sofia and others have given their approval to share these stories we experienced. So please do not feel as though I would share such personal experiences without the approval of others that were involved.

Before we get started, I want to give you a thought. I believe I found this on Facebook, but it did not list who penned this. I do not take credit, but it certainly is powerful.

"The most free person in the world is the one who has nothing to hide."

I told you how I love quotes and music. If you want to be blessed, I encourage you to go online and listen to the following song. I believe this is a wonderful song to accompany this chapter because it makes me think of what I've been through and how I want to help others find the hope and healing they might need:

"Scars"

-By: I Am They

Chapter 2

Innocence Lost: The Need For Parameters
Trauma: The Beginning Of Harmful
Thought Processes

As I am sitting here in my office at my home, I will tell you that this is not what I had written down in my notes to begin writing about at this point. I experienced hardships prior to this incident, but I feel I need to start here. As I look back, though, I do believe this is where my life took a real turn for the worse and started to spiral out of control. So, in essence, I guess it is the perfect place to begin with sharing my story.

Let me paint for you a picture of what my pre-teen years were like. Immediately after my 10th birthday, my family moved out to a small, rural town. I was devastated. I loved the suburban town we had lived in from the time I was born until my 10th birthday. I could not stand the idea of leaving all I knew. I had tons of friends in our neighborhood. I went to a great school. My Nannie and Grandaddy (my dad's parents) lived next door to us. My Aunt Janie and Uncle Morris and their kids lived right next to my grandparents. And my great-grandmother, Granny Harper, lived right next door to them. I was surrounded by family and friends. I was happy. I was content. I was safe. Life was good. Then we moved.

Now, I was not a selfish, bratty 10-year-old. I was just sad to leave the only life I had known. Also, I was scared to move out to the country and start over in a place that seemed like Mars to my little mind. My mom had grown up in this town. My dad had always wanted a farm with a bunch of land and cattle. They were excited. Us kids, not so much. So much so that my brother Dean, who was old enough, made the decision to use my grandparents' address and finish up his schooling in the town we previously lived in. Being 10, I did not have a driver's license, so no chance of that happening for me.

I remember the day we were taken out to our new home. I could not believe my eyes. My parents had bought 88 acres of land down a dirt road with two dilapidated barns, a well for water, a house that had not been lived in for two years and had been deemed "uninhabitable." It was falling apart. Yeh! This was my new home. On top of that, we had six people in our family, and this was a two-bedroom house. We continuously had to go to our old house, which was on the market for sale, to fill milk containers with drinking water because the water at this new house came from a well and was brown. We had to bathe in this dirty, dark water, but you could not drink it. Let's go ahead and throw one more curveball in the mix: the house was infested with scorpions…stinging scorpions. We had to wear shoes at all times just in case any of us stepped on a scorpion. You did not want to get stung by one of these little devils. What is even worse is they could crawl onto the ceiling and fall into bed with you and sting you. That never happened to me because I had a canopy bed, but more than one family member experienced that middle-of-the-night pain. Rats and mice were an issue as well. Snakes? Yes, of course. The house was overgrown with bushes and just totally unkept. I could not believe this was our new home. I was sad, scared. And I was just expected to move on in life like this was the greatest adventure ever. Not.

My first day of school was not the greatest. I don't exactly know what I was expecting. It was an old school with just one building that housed kindergarten through 12th grade. I was terrified. I was unhappy. I was the new kid. And to top it off, the most popular boy in class asked me to be his girlfriend the first day I was there, so now I was the most hated girl in class. For a time, two of the popular girls in class kind of verbally abused me a bit. One day during P.E. class, I was upset, and these girls asked me why I just didn't go back to where I came from. It was a rough beginning.

Things eventually got better at school. The house issue was just misery. There is no other word to describe the situation and how I felt. My oldest brother, Vance, was literally sleeping on the screened back porch as his room. This may be a good time to mention that I am the youngest of four children. My oldest brother is Vance. My middle brother is Dean. My youngest brother is Kevin. I am the baby girl. My dad knew he had four able-bodied kids. My dad was also a driven man. Over time he designed a simple layout for adding on to this old farmhouse. And his four children were put to work doing what we could. Now, I am not against having your kids help out around the house, but I remember being scared as I was on the second story of this addition nailing down black tarp before the roofers came. We built all that we could personally do ourselves. We still had to have electricians, plumbers, and roofers come out to make everything code and take care of the projects that our family was not equipped to handle. By the time it was complete, the two-bedroom farmhouse that was falling apart at the seams became a two-story, six-bedroom home where everyone had their own space. But it took years to get to that point. It was emotionally hard. It was physically hard. I think it took a toll on my family in many ways.

The school issue continued to improve. And those two girls that had been mean to me eventually became friends of mine. Tough times during elementary school came to pass. Eventually, the town added a new high school building, and things were a bit happier. I made cheerleader at the end of my 7th grade year, which would put me being an 8th grade cheerleader. I remember getting the news that I had made the squad. It was one of the happiest moments in my life up until that point. But the happy moments were continually overshadowed by things that were going on in the background… things that were out of my control. Things that would eventually cause my thoughts and actions to supersede wisdom. Situations that made me deal with issues I should not even have had to deal with as a kid.

Obviously, I will not be able to communicate every single one of the details that transpired as I was growing up. However, I can give you a good idea of incidents and episodes that began to take a very negative hold on my young life. My oldest brother, Vance, who was my protector when I was a baby, eventually became a nightmare to me and my family. He started growing weed on my parent's property, drinking way too much, using illegal drugs, stealing, getting into trouble at school, getting in worse trouble with law enforcement, disobedient towards my parents, belligerent…you name it. He just became a mean person. I remember one time he got mad at me because I wouldn't answer the phone, and he chased me through the house. I ran into my room and locked the door, but he busted it down and threw me up against the wall and was holding me up by my neck. I was choking. He was cussing at me. Eventually, he just dropped me and left. Even though my family did not go to church, I now look back and say God was protecting me that day because Vance had pure hate in his eyes towards me. I did not think I had done anything wrong to receive that type of treatment. It was crazy. There is no other way to say it other than Vance was a juvenile delinquent. His actions and deeds were heartbreaking to my parents, and they could not control him. But time and time again, they bailed him out of trouble. I never understood that. Vance caused tension, and I was afraid of him. Being at home had its challenges.

Furthermore, to add to that, my youngest brother Kevin started drinking and getting into trouble at school and with the law. Kevin was not violent like Vance, but he did pick on me to extremes. I can remember one thing he seemed to enjoy doing was tackling me, then straddling me and pinning me down by pressing his knees on top of my shoulders so I could not move or fight back. Then he would either tap my chest bone until it hurt or spit in my face. My brothers also enjoyed getting great laughs at my expense by saying things like I was a pirate's dream because of my "sunken chest." I was not endowed in the chest area, and they continually made fun of me. It made me feel "less-than" and unattractive.

I know all siblings probably fight, but some things that happened to me were damaging to my developing mind. My reason for sharing these experiences is so you will get an idea of what my home life was like and the ramifications of the actions against me. I was a "good girl." But due to the reputations of Vance and Kevin, I was labeled a "bad girl." I was not involved or taking part in the things they were doing. But it did not seem to matter. Some adults in our small country town made me guilty by association.

I wasn't anything like Vance and Kevin. But do you have any idea of how hard it was when my friend's parents wouldn't allow them to come to my house because of the exploits of my brothers? It crushed me. Being a parent myself now, I understand the decision they made. But I didn't then. I was just an innocent kid. It hurt. Do you know how it feels when you have been referred to as a "slut," even when you were still a virgin? Do you know what it feels like to be judged because of other people's actions?

My brothers' lifestyles and choices ruined my reputation. Many of the adults in our community just considered me a bad seed. Luckily, the kids in our school knew I was nothing like my brothers. As I mentioned, I was a cheerleader, I did drill team, I was FFA Sweetheart one year, I was Football Sweetheart one year. Those are the things that kept me hanging on. Why did I need something to hang onto? Because there were even teachers and administration staff at the school that mistreated me due to my brothers. The principal did not care for me, but the Superintendent was a sweet, kind man, and he never looked at me with darkened eyes. He knew I was not like my brothers. I was just in a bad situation. So in the chaos of my school years, God allowed a few silver linings in that gave me hope to rise above what was going on around me and in my community. Vance and Kevin both graduated, and things got a little better. Unfortunately, the damage was already done.

My senior year in high school was a huge turning point for me. I had started drinking some. Alcohol was always easy to get. Everyone had older friends or, yes, even parents who would buy alcoholic beverages for us. I would like to note that my entire school experience wasn't all horrible. I did have friends and fun but a lot of problems to deal with as well. Problems that should have never been mine to deal with. By the time I was a senior in high school, I believe my parents were so worn out by everything that Vance and Kevin had put them through that my parents had just given up. I had no rules.

I had no boundaries. I had no restrictions or consequences. Additionally, I had no role model, mentor, or scope of reality in a sense. I felt like my parents were almost absent from my life at times. They were there but not there. I felt no emotional support. My dad had always been a workaholic. He had his own business that he ran during the day, then in the evening, he would come home and farm. Our mom was pretty much our mom and our dad, so she was worn thin. They were, and are, good parents. They provided for our needs. We were taken care of. I just didn't feel the emotional support I needed. There were times I felt like I was raising myself. This was not a good situation to be in.

With the absence of parental guidance or control, I started drinking and partying a little more. I hadn't really dated because my brothers were over-protective of me in that one area. One example would be when a boy, who was a senior, asked me to the prom when I was a freshman in high school. I was excited and scared all at the same time. I had not even kissed a boy. But on the night of the prom, Vance met my date at the door, with a rifle in hand, and told this young man not to lay a hand on me and not to even think about kissing me goodnight. True story. Just ask Vance or my mom. Needless to say, boys didn't really ask me out much. My brothers were big and had a reputation, as you know. I mean, I would have a "boyfriend" from time to time that was a relationship that consisted of passing notes in school, hanging out at school events, and talking on the phone. That's about it.

Then it happened. I had made it to my senior year of high school. Senior year comes with a flurry of excitement and emotions. I was glad to begin my last year of school, but I was also facing adulthood and all the responsibilities that came with that. During this time, I met a guy through a friend. He and I started talking. We started liking each other. I had no business getting involved with this guy. He was in his early 20s. I was 17. But he "saw" me. He asked me questions about myself. He didn't judge me. And the fact that my dad was a present but absent figure in my life, this man made me feel important, pretty, and likable. That's a dangerous combination for a young girl that often felt invisible. Plus, this young man had a cool sports car that he let me drive and take my friends out in. Once again, I had no business dating this older guy but no one to tell me not to. By this time, I had developed a little bit of a rebellious side. I was still a sweet young girl, but there was so much I didn't know about life. I was emotionally immature, which led me to make some bad decisions. One of those bad decisions was going to this young man's apartment one night. A night I will never forget.

I do not recall if he and I had gone out to eat or to a movie or what happened prior to going to his apartment. I can still see in my mind what the outside of his apartment building looked like. I remember I had on a pretty dress. I remember kissing him. I remember cuddling with him. And I remember that I just "froze" as things got out of hand. I don't remember much after that. I don't even remember him driving me home. I just remember feeling lost and dirty. I was 17. I had every intention of saving myself for my future husband. That had been taken from me.

I wish I could say that night was the end of it, but it wasn't. In my broken childlike state, not knowing what to do and not having an adult in my life to turn to, I went out with this guy a couple more times. Why? I don't know. I guess because he had what I had been saving for my future husband, so I, in some messed up state of mind, thought I needed to try and make things "work" with this guy. But things were different. Obviously. He asked me what was wrong. I told him that I was a virgin before what had happened at his apartment. His reply was, "You weren't a virgin! You didn't even bleed!" I shot back at him that I had been a virgin and that I didn't know why I hadn't bled. I didn't even know how he possibly enjoyed it because I just froze and did nothing.

I need to further explain something with regards to the fact that I "did nothing." I have heard several other rape stories over the years. Many of these women thought it was their fault because they did not fight back. They froze, just like I did. Recently I was helping Sofia register for a college class. She is 15 years old, but she wants to graduate early. She is taking dual credit courses for high school and college. In order for her to proceed with the registration, she was required to watch some videos and answer questions afterward. The videos are a state requirement for all students prior to registering for college courses. It is called #NotAnymore Training, and it consists of a series of videos about college, alcohol, what is inappropriate behavior, precautions to take, and rape. I loved what so much of the series had to say, but the thing that caught my attention, and a very important truth, is one specific line that stated, *"If someone isn't actively participating, it's not consent. It's rape."* So, if someone reading this froze or didn't fight back, if you were under the influence of any substance, it's not your fault; it's rape.

My mind did not know how to comprehend what had happened to me. I did not know how to handle all the emotions that I was experiencing. But I was a senior in high school, and time and life marched on. I had schoolwork. I had friends. I had plans. My life was ahead of me. But then I started feeling sick. At first, I thought I just had a bug that was going around. But it wasn't going away. I was sick to my stomach often. I just did not feel right. It was at that time that a horrifying thought entered my mind. I went to a clinic and had a pregnancy test done. I could not believe it when I heard the words, "You're pregnant." What? I was terrified.

I want to take a moment to interject that my brother Dean, the one who never got in trouble, started going to our local community church during my early years of high school. After a while, I started going with him. Eventually, I started going on my own. We were the only two people in my family that were attending church. Mom had taken us to some when we were little kids, but then we just quit going. But I was back. And I had decided the Christian life was for me.

Being a Christian had everything to do with me wanting to save myself for marriage. It did not keep me from drinking here and there and getting a little rebellious at times. The point I want to make is that I was a Christian at this stage in my life, and I knew right from wrong. And in my faith, I believe that life begins at conception. So regardless of the fact that I became pregnant during a sexual assault that took my virginity, I believed in my heart that abortion was wrong.

The sickness did not go away. I had been trying to manage going to school and feeling ill. I tried not to think about how I lost my virginity. I tried not to think about being pregnant. But those two things could not be ignored. I felt like my life was spiraling out of control. I was sad, distraught, emotionally battered, and didn't want anyone to know what had happened to me…what was happening to me. But then I got angry. I let something else take control over me. And the saddest part of all is that I could no longer make rational decisions. At that point, I could no longer see the tiny, innocent, living baby inside of me as what it was…a precious, innocent life. I saw it as something that would keep me connected to the man who raped me for the rest of my life. Common sense was gone. Hurt and anger overshadowed the truth. The truth that the child inside of me deserved to live. Sadly, in my broken state, I just wanted nothing to keep me connected to "that man." He already stole my innocence. I could never get that back. I could never share that with my future husband. My only thought was that I could not have the baby. No one even knew what had happened to me. I did not want people to know that I was no longer a virgin. I did not want to be with this man. Every time I looked at him, I felt hurt. I felt resentment. In my broken, messed up 17-year-old mind, all I could think was that I had to sweep all of this under the rug. No one knew. No one needed to know. Life would go on. That man took my innocence, but I could not let what he did to me steal my reputation and my life as well. My thought was I could not be connected to him for the rest of my life. I could not have this baby.

Before moving forward, if you have experienced neglect or emotional or physical abuse of any kind, let me validate you by saying abuse is never okay. Never. At the time we actually go through and experience these things, the pain does not stop once it is over. These types of traumatic experiences can have a lasting effect on your life if it is not dealt with. We tend to think once the abuse has stopped, we are all better. We are safe. Life goes on. In my own life, the trauma was just the beginning. My mind became my biggest enemy.

I felt neglected, overlooked, unimportant, and dirty. What's worse is the fact that the way you view yourself can lead to unhealthy habits, bad decisions, and isolation. Then the worst of all is that you may not even realize this is going on within your head. I believe the biggest thing I have learned while going through therapy is that there are things that leave a traumatic impact on our lives that we never even recognized as trauma. Harsh words spoken, a parent forgetting to pick you up from school, a lost friendship, and so forth. If these things left an impact on your life in a negative way, it was traumatic. It is not just the "big things" that cause trauma. This concept will make more sense as we go through the book. Even keeping secrets can negatively affect you and the way you think and act and respond to things and people.

Nobody knew what I was going through. But God knew. Even though I was blinded to His presence because of the pain, He was with me through it all. I want you to know there is hope. There is healing. There is. As I continue with my story, please know that what happens to us in life is not who we are. Injustice is not our fault but taking steps towards healing is our responsibility. We were never meant to just merely exist. Life is ours for the taking, for the living.

"God Only Knows"

-By: For King and Country

Chapter 3

One Abortion: Two Lives Gone
One Truth: God's Grace Is Bigger Than
My Mistakes

I knew of a family friend, another teenager, that had gone through with an abortion. I recalled the name of the doctor that had performed her procedure. In Texas, you are considered an adult at the age of 17, so I did not need my parent's permission to proceed with an abortion. This seemed like the best way out of my situation because I did not want my parents or anyone else to know what had happened to me or what I was planning on doing.

I remember going to the appointment. I remember thinking that I would have never in a thousand years thought I would ever be in the situation I was in. I never imagined I would be in a place to make this type of decision. And it was a decision. It was a choice. But I felt like I had no other choice. I already felt "dirty" and "used" from the sexual assault. Now I was having to deal with the guilt of what I was doing. What I most regret is that no one even tried to talk me out of it. No one told me my options. I was an emotionally wrecked kid, and everyone in that doctor's office was business as usual. Happy-go-lucky. *We are here to serve you. Let's take care of this problem. Life will go on. You're all good. You will be fine afterward.* All lies.

I don't know how the procedure takes place today, but 35 years ago, it was a 2-day process. What? I could not believe I would have to come back another day. At my first visit, the medical staff "prepped" me. Afterward, I went home. I was in emotional pain and physical pain from something they had inserted in me. But here's the clincher. I was told that when I came back the next day, someone would have to come with me. My only thought was, "What?" Due to the fact that I had to be put to sleep for the abortion, the doctor could not release me after the procedure unless I had someone to drive me home. No exceptions! I thought, "What now? How is this going to happen?" I was totally freaking out. Crying. What else could go wrong in my life? Wrong question to ask.

I knew I had very little time to decide what to do. I had to be back at the doctor's office for the abortion procedure the next day. Who would take me? Who could I trust? My secrets were unfolding. Who would help me sweep all of this under the rug so I could go on and live a normal life afterward? There was only one answer. And I knew it. My mom. I did not know how I was going to tell her what had happened to me. I did not know how I could tell her I was no longer a virgin. I had no idea how she would react when I told her that I was pregnant. What would she say when I asked her to be my driver in order to go and have an abortion?

Right at this moment, I need to just pause and pray. This is hard. Not what I am telling you about me. There are plenty of people that know my story. But no one knew that my mom was a part of it. My ex-husband, David, and my psychologist both know, but other than the two of them, it has not been public knowledge. Until now.

I remember trembling as I called my mom into the bedroom so we could talk in private. I do not remember the exact words I spoke to her, but when I was done talking…and crying my way through it…mom was aware of what had happened with this young man and that I was pregnant as a result. She also knew I had planned an abortion and needed a driver. I am sure my story was a lot to take in. It was also a lot to let come out of my mouth. If I remember correctly, I looked into a blank face. Mom agreed to be my driver. And the only other thing I remember clear as day is her saying, "Your father can never know about this. It would kill him!" I agreed to her request. And that was the end of that conversation.

After years of counseling, I now know that this encounter was a pivotal, ongoing, life-changing moment in my life. I need you to grasp what just happened here. At 17, I had to face my biggest fear and go to my mother and let her know that I had been raped, that I was pregnant, and that I needed her to drive me to get an abortion. I was scared. I was still dealing with all the hurt and anguish that came with what had happened and what I was going through. And the thing that stuck in my mind was my mom's demand that no one, especially my dad, ever know about this. What I needed was a long, tear-drenched hug. I needed to hear that maybe I should take some time to think about it and consider other options. I needed someone to tell me I was still okay. I needed someone to tell me that this was not all my fault. I needed the pain to just go away. I needed my mom to just be there for me. As a result of the conversation between the two of us, something happened that turned my world upside down and would contribute to so many wrong decisions in my life. Because after my mom's comments, two things began to overtake me and subsequently somewhat took control of my life: Guilt and Shame.

"GUILT tells me I've done something wrong. But SHAME tells me I AM something wrong."

-Sheila Walsh, Author, Speaker, Teacher, Television Host

You need to go back and read that again. It is very powerful. I did not know it then, but that day, so many years ago when I was a mere 17-year-old "damaged" young girl, when I needed validation for my life and what I was feeling, shame entered my life, and its roots went deep, quickly. I wish I could stop here and personally speak face to face with everyone reading this that might possibly be dealing with shame. Although I am not there with you, let me tell you shame is not who you are. You are not "something wrong." Shame is something that happened to you. Shame is too heavy of a load for you to carry. Shame twists the thoughts you have about yourself. Shame also makes you question how others perceive you. Shame is a liar.

I know I am interrupting the story, but I must share this right now. Years after this event between my mom and me took place, I noticed that I predominately walked everywhere I went looking at the ground. Head bent down. That's shame. One day I was out on a walk, and I heard God say, "Eyes up." I was like, "What?" God so tenderly told me that I had spent most of my life walking around, looking down. He reminded me that I had asked for forgiveness for my decisions, and I was forgiven. God told me I needed to walk in that forgiveness. Stride after stride. Step after step. Eyes up! I will never forget that day. I hope you grasp this and know you need not hold your head down in shame. God's grace is limitless, and shame has no place in our lives.

Back to where I left off. Even though I was not aware of this fact when I was 17, what happened between my mom and me was the point in my life that I believe I stopped liking me. I started feeling ugly, invisible, unworthy, unlikable, and so many other things. Don't get me wrong. I had some wonderful, great, happy times throughout my life, but this ugly little monster of shame was always lurking in the back shadows of my mind and controlled so many of the decisions I made. Not good.

For anyone thinking poorly of my mom, please don't. My mom had no idea how impactful her reaction was to me. I was a very strong-willed young girl. And my mom knew that. I do not believe my mom knew how to deal with this situation. She probably just thought that if an abortion was what I had decided to do, then that was what we would do. My mom is an amazing person. You will find out more about my mom in a later chapter. More that will help understand why she wasn't there for me when I needed her to be during this critical time in my life.

I really do not remember a whole lot about the day of the abortion. I do remember waking up in the procedure room. I was alone. I was disoriented. I remember walking down the hall in my hospital gown, spaced out, blood running down my legs, and a nurse running up to me and escorting me back to my room. Evidently, I had woken up sooner than they had anticipated. I don't mean to offend anyone by being so graphic, but I just want you to realize what I remember. And I remember being walked back to my room to get cleaned up, and the only thought going through my head was, "I just killed a part of me."

Back then, I had no idea what a profound impact that thought would have on my life. It was true. True in two ways. Without a doubt, I had just taken the life of the innocent little baby that was inside of me. But I had just taken my life as well. The guilt and shame consumed me in a way that I cannot even explain. In a matter of a few short months, my life had been flipped upside down, and I began to drown. I was not okay. I did not feel fine after the procedure. Life did not go back to normal. Everything that was told to me at that doctor's office was a lie.

Mom and I didn't talk about that day. At least not for a long time. We just kind of acted like it never happened. I ended contact with the guy. I did tell him what I had done. He didn't seem too bothered by it. I guess his life did go on.

Before I go on to the next chapter, I want to mention a few things here and share a few quotes. If you have ever been the victim of a sexual assault, rape is never okay. If you think it was your fault, it wasn't. I could strip down naked and walk down the street or into a bar, but that still does not give any person the thumbs up to force himself on me. If you feel guilty, don't. I am not here to try and brush off your pain. I am here to validate it. What happened to you was wrong. But do not let it steal your life. You have lost enough. You deserve better. And if you have had an abortion and feel shame or guilt, don't. I am not here to justify your actions. But I am here to tell you that Jesus died on a cross to take away all our sins, shame, brokenness, and more. Ask for His forgiveness and receive it. That may be easy for me to say all these years later, but I think you will understand when we get further into my story. No, I feel God leading me to share this now, so I will follow His leading as He knows better than me.

I will begin this by saying that what I am about to share with you does not "line up" with modern or ancient theology. But I know for a fact that this happened, and if you have had an abortion, then maybe, just maybe, it will help you receive the forgiveness that God so openly and graciously offers. Up until just a few years ago, I thought I was "free" from the guilt I carried over having an abortion. Several times over the years, I would be at a conference or a church service, and something would happen that would make me think I was free from all the feelings of guilt and unworthiness, but something was always still in the back of my mind. Shame and guilt still had so much control over me and my emotions and actions.

It was Sunday, January 22, 2017. David and I were at church in Garland, Texas. At that time, David was serving as Associate Pastor at the church we were attending. Our daughters, Sofia and Lily, were in Sunday school classes. That day, there was a visiting pastor speaking at our church. This pastor was a longtime friend of David's. His name is Kevin Bates, and he pastors a church in Louisiana. I wrote all about that day in my journal. I didn't want to forget one moment of that day. The sermon Kevin preached was called "The Great Exchange." The message was about the life of Job. If you are not familiar with the story of Job in the Bible, it is worth the read. So much so that it is an entire book of the Bible. Bottom line, Job was a wealthy, respected family man of influence among his people. Satan told God that he believed he could get Job to curse God and turn from Him. God allowed Satan to have his way with Job, but God told Satan that he could not take Job's life. Long story short, Satan inflicted total chaos and havoc on Job. Satan destroyed all of Job's livestock, possessions and caused the deaths of all his children. Then Job was struck with a deadly disease, and he was covered all over his body with terrible boils. I will not go further in the story other than to say that Job was a man of upright character that loved God. And although Job questioned God, he never cursed God as Satan had hoped for. In the end, God restored all that had been taken from Job and more. The book of Job seems like a horrible story, but it is truly one of hope, redemption, and restoration.

Back to the highlights of Kevin's message, "The Great Exchange." Kevin explained that an exchange is when something is taken away from you, but something else is given back in return for what was taken…something of greater value. God does not cause things we perceive as bad to happen in our lives. But He does allow them. God does not take away unless He is going to give something back that is better. When Kevin started listing everything that had been taken away from Job, yet Job still loved God, I was fine. I was just sitting in the congregation and taking it all in. Then, Pastor Kevin spoke of the seven sons and three daughters that were taken away from Job, and I started tearing up and became overcome with emotion. Kevin continued with the sermon, but I began thinking about my two abortions (yes, we will get to that later). My two children that were taken from me.

Now I know some people may say that my two children were not "taken" from me…that I made a conscious decision to abort each child. I am not going to argue about that because it is correct. At the same time, I was not in my right mind. I was too young to make such decisions, was broken from being raped, and so many other things that we will get into later. Satan loves to have a heyday with our minds. I do not discard what I did, but the enemy had a huge part in the decisions I made, and I will leave it at that.

I was mourning the loss of my children. Kevin had already been preaching that NOTHING happens without God's foreknowledge. Any and everything that happens in your life that you perceive as bad, God already knew it was going to happen and allowed it to happen. Most people would say my two abortions were my choice. And up until that day in January 2017, I would have told you the exact same thing. But something finally broke in me that morning at church. I had thought I was free from shame and guilt, but I wasn't…until that day.

Again, as Kevin was talking about the children that were taken from Job, and I was thinking about the loss of my two children, I heard a still, small voice. I totally and clearly heard God say to me in my spirit, "They volunteered!" I knew exactly what God meant, but He said it again, "They volunteered!" God knew that He had to get this truth into the deepest recesses of my mind, my spirit, and my heart, "They volunteered." Some people may not get this or agree with it, but I knew what God was imparting to me. Immediately, my mind was taken to the scripture that says:

"You made all the delicate, inner parts of my body

and knit me together in my mother's womb.

Thank you for making me so wonderfully complex!

Your workmanship is marvelous—how well I know it.

You watched me as I was being formed in utter seclusion,

As I was woven together in the dark of the womb.

You saw me before I was born.

Every day of my life was recorded in your book.

Every moment was laid out

before a single day had passed."

--Psalm 139:13-16 (NLT)

This spoke several things to me. I was just crying. It was like the heaviness and burden that I had carried for so many years had finally been lifted off me. God knew us before we were born. Does that mean we existed before we took human form in the womb of a woman? I am sure theologians would argue against me. And that is fine. Because in the end, it does not matter. What matters to me is what was spoken into my spirit, whether it is theologically correct or not. What it spoke to me was that my two children existed in spirit and were with God. They knew they would be terminated and never be born into this world but, "They volunteered" because they knew they would return to God and there was no other place they would rather be, so there was no fear on their part. In my spirit, I also felt they did it out of love for me and their two future sisters, Sofia and Lily. If my first two children had been born, Sofia would have never existed, and I would have never adopted

Lily. My life would have been completely different. They gave their lives for Sofia, Lily, and me. Why? I can't say for sure, but Kevin said in his sermon that God took away Job's "first" (children) but established or exchanged them for the "miraculous" (children). Sofia was born handicapped, and Lily was born with a life-threatening disease, but God healed both of my children. Doctors can't even explain the miraculous change of health in Sofia and Lily. I will share their stories later in this book. If you do not believe in miracles, you just might after you hear what God did in Sofia and Lily's lives. The point here is that the first two children could not stay if the second two were to be my children. "They volunteered."

I am not saying this is doctrine. I have read the Bible from cover to cover many times and continue to read my Bible. There is nothing in the Bible to validate nor disprove what I am sharing as truth or not. But I am saying I know what I heard in my spirit. And I know that something broke off me that day, and I have never again felt guilt or shame regarding the rape or the abortions. That kind of healing and freedom does not just happen on its own. God's hand was in that. To me, when I heard they volunteered, this scripture came to mind:

"For the greatest love of all is a love that sacrifices all. And this great love is demonstrated when a person sacrifices his life for his friends."

-John 15:13 (TPT)

The Aramaic word for friends refers to family or relatives. I know what I heard. I know the total love that surrounded me. I was finally able to accept and receive forgiveness. Thirty years of guilt and shame was stripped off me in an instant. Why did it take so long? I do not know. Why did it happen that particular day? I do not know. What I do know is that I felt like I could breathe again. The guilt and shame of my past no longer had a grip on me. Thank you, God!

One more amazing part of Pastor Kevin's sermon was when Kevin pointed out that God restored everything to Job. He restored Job's wealth, possessions, and so forth. God multiplied everything that had been taken from Job…everything but the number of children. Previously Job had seven sons and three daughters that had been killed, but God gave Job another seven sons and three daughters. Why didn't God "double" the payback here? Because Job didn't really "lose" his first ten children. They still exist; they are with God. I could not even speak after this sermon. Tears were flowing as the floodgate of healing, peace, joy, love, and freedom flooded my heart, mind, and spirit. I shared all of this with David after church that day, and he could even see the difference in me. People think they have God figured out. They don't. I don't. But I love it when He unveils a little something about Himself, and we get to see a little piece of heaven right here on earth.

If you have had an abortion, or multiple abortions, and you just cannot seem to forgive yourself, just let it go. Guilt and shame are too heavy of burdens for you to carry. God does not want you to be stuck in an unhealthy pattern of the "What ifs." You have been weighted down for too long. Receive the forgiveness, grace, and love that God is extending to you. There is not a doubt in my mind that I will see the two children I aborted in heaven one day, and that moment will be a glorious encounter.

If you are struggling emotionally as a result of an abortion, please talk to someone. I would like to add that abortion does not only affect women. Men encounter feelings of guilt or even anger at the loss of their child. These feelings are natural. These feelings are also harmful. Please do not assume you do not need to talk through these feelings with someone you can trust. The loss of a child is traumatic regardless of how that life was lost. But you can heal.

Worship music is my warship. Throughout the last ten years or so of my life, there are certain songs that bring me into the presence of God, and His love surrounds me. If you ever need a bit of encouragement and reassurance of God's love for you, no matter what you have done in life, you might want to hop online and check out these songs:

"Redeemed"

-By: Big Daddy Weave

"He Loves Us"

-By: David Crowder Band

"Rescue"

-By: Lauren Daigle

I would also like to share some quotes that I hope will bring some peace, encouragement, hope, or whatever you need to find healing and restoration. The first one I am going to share I just heard this past week. We were taping a show with Joni Eareckson Tada. If you don't know her, please research her. When Joni was 17 years old, she was injured in a diving accident that left her a quadriplegic. She is now 71 years old and has led a life of struggle and inspiration. Her face just beams with the love of God. During her time with us during taping, she talked about her life and her love for God through it all. She made this striking statement that stuck with me:

"God permits what He hates, always to accomplish that which He loves."

-Joni Eareckson Tada, Author, Speaker, Overcomer

Joni added that *"suffering pushes us against the cross."* Basically, this takes us back to the story of Job. God doesn't make bad things happen to us, but He does allow bad things to happen to us. Like Joni said, He permits what He hates. Why? Because it forms Christ in us, and that is God's goal. He loves that! For so many years, I was angry with God for not protecting me, protecting my innocence. I was a "good girl." Why should I have gotten raped? For years I was mad at my parents. Why didn't they give me rules and boundaries? If they had, I would not have been dating an older guy. I would not have been raped. I would not have been faced with an unwanted pregnancy by the man who raped me. For years, I was angry with me. Why did I make such stupid choices that had horrific consequences that changed my life and sent me down a road of self-hate, anger, bitterness, depression, promiscuity, and alcohol just trying to numb the pain? Why do so many people have easy lives, and mine was filled with so much hurt? These were not the questions I should have been asking. I will get into that story a little bit later.

I do know a few things, though. I survived. I became a very independent and strong person, but those weren't always good traits. I never played the victim. The majority of my anger was directed at me. It is said that the Lord never gives us more than we can handle. There were many times I questioned that in my own life. But God knew what was inside of Job, his strength, tenacity, and devotion to God. And God knew Job could handle what he was about to go through. Otherwise, God would not have permitted it to happen. God knew Job would not only survive but live to thrive. It has taken me over 30 years to overcome my past, but not only did I survive, I am also thriving. I won't lie, though; many things were very hard along the way. I don't believe that it is the easy things that shape who we become, and I love who I am now. It is up to you to decide what your life will speak about you and who you will allow your life to mold you into. Open your eyes and see the truth of the amazing potential that resides within you.

Before we move forward, I want to share some quotes that might make you think and inspire you in some way.

"Hurt and hope can co-exist. Shame is the scheme of the enemy to hold us down mentally and emotionally from everything God has for us, on the other side of healing. Shame is an identity snatcher. Thieves don't steal from empty houses. We all have something of value inside of us."

-Toni Collier, Author, Communicator, Host, Consultant

"Grace isn't about having a second chance; grace is having so many chances that you could use all through all eternity and never come up empty. It's when you finally realize that the other shoe isn't going to drop, ever."

-Shauna Niequist, Author, Speaker

"You have to walk now when you don't have a picture of what God has for you. God is for you, but if you're not careful, Satan will trick you into believing God wants you hurting. But God is fighting for us."

- Aly & Josh Taylor, Authors and Speakers

"Out of suffering have emerged the strongest souls; the most massive characters are seared with scars."

-Khalil Gibran

I also want to tell you that pain isolates us, and your emotions will lie to you. I lost so much in life due to guilt and shame. Please do not allow the same thing to happen in your life. God has so much more for you.

"You're Gonna Be Ok"

-By: Brian & Jenn Johnson

Chapter 4

Losing My Mind
Gaining Clarity

I realize that I ended the previous chapter on a happy note. God is not at all allowing me to follow the outline that I had prepared for this book. I was going to share all the heartache and pain, then show how God turned it all around. But evidently, this is the direction that I am supposed to be going, and I am good with that. Or, in the words of Zig Ziglar, *"Better than good."*

Something snapped in me after the first abortion. I was no longer me. I had to act like what I had been through had never happened. I had to paint on a happy face and move forward. I had to finish high school and figure out what I was going to do with my life. My life? What did that even mean anymore? My mind was not right. My emotions were all over the place. I felt completely out of control. I felt fake. I felt like a liar. I felt ugly. I did not know how to let go of the pain. I cried. And no one had a clue that any of this was going on. I had become a pro at burying my pain. I had no one to talk to. I did not really want to talk about it, any of it, anyway. But I must tell you something that is of great importance. You do not bury something that is not dead. And my pain was very much alive.

So, what happened? I turned into the very person some adults in my small town had accused me of being. I started drinking to numb the pain. I started partying. I never did drugs, though. I saw what drugs had done to my oldest brother, and that terrified me. Alcohol was my drug of choice. I started going to clubs, dancing until the wee hours of the morning. I did graduate from high school, but I did not go directly into college. My last year of high school was not my fondest, so I felt I needed a break. That was inevitably a big mistake. I needed something to focus on…something to keep me busy. But partying with my friends seemed like more fun…from what I can remember of it.

I met a guy…a really nice, good guy. I grew up in a small town 20 minutes out of Waco, Texas. There is a strip of road that goes through part of Waco called Valley Mills Drive. And on the weekends, kids from towns all over "cruised the valley." It was the thing teenagers did back then. One night I was with some friends, and I saw this cute guy on a motorcycle, a racing motorcycle at that, parked in a parking lot. My friend John knew this guy. I asked John if he thought this guy would take me riding on his bike. John yelled for the guy to come over, and he did. Remember now that I had buried my past and acted normal. John introduced me to this guy, and he took me riding on the motorcycle. He was so kind and sweet. He was also very careful and didn't try any crazy stunts while I was on the bike with him. I felt safe with him. When he took me back to where my friends were, he asked me for my phone number, and I gave it to him.

We started dating and became boyfriend and girlfriend pretty quickly. He was the perfect gentleman. But as the dating progressed, we were in a situation and mutually agreed to take our relationship further. You can imagine his surprise when he first touched me, and I immediately froze and started crying uncontrollably. He just looked at me and asked, "What did he do to you?" He knew something had happened. I told him about the rape, and he just held me…the one thing I had needed ever since that horrible night.

We eventually did become intimate. I never freaked out again after that first night. He made me feel protected and cared for. And that is what I had needed for so many years. We dated for quite a while. He had even bought me a promise ring. I don't know if guys still do that type of thing these days. It was a ring to signify his promise to me to be faithful and to replace that ring with an engagement ring someday. I still think that is the sweetest and most romantic gesture.

I wish I could say things continued to be blissful and beautiful between us, but then it happened…again. I started feeling sick. I didn't have to guess. I knew all too well what this feeling probably meant. Why hadn't we been more careful? STUPID! STUPID! STUPID ME! I went in for a pregnancy test, and yes, again, I found myself pregnant. Instead of being strong and moving forward. Instead of being strong and sharing this news with this sweet, sweet boyfriend of mine. Instead of being strong and thinking logically, I regressed back into "fix it" mode without even thinking it through and made the appointment.

I had no logical "reason" for aborting this baby. I was happy. I was with a good guy that wanted to marry me someday. But it's like I went into this fog, and I automatically resorted to what I had done before. But it was different this time. Unfortunately, for some reason, I didn't see that it was different. I had the abortion without even telling the guy. That was wrong. He deserved to know. At that time, in a matter of less than two years, I had been raped and had two abortions. Without a doubt, this was pretty much what sent me over the edge. My two adversaries, guilt and shame, were right up in my face again. My time of happiness with a good guy had passed. I ended up dumping him because I could not face him about what I had done behind his back. He was completely hurt and bewildered. He had no idea how we went from a happy couple to nothing. He tried to find out why I had left, but I wouldn't tell him. I quickly started dating someone else so he would just think I was a loser because that was what I felt like. But it was a cop-out. It was sorry. He didn't deserve that.

All common sense had left me by this time. I could not in any logical way deal with what had happened to me in the past, and I could not outrun the feelings that were overtaking me. I started leading a very self-destructive lifestyle. I had thoughts of suicide, but my previous time in church, which I had left by now, had at least grounded me enough to know that suicide was never the answer. I drank. I partied. I became promiscuous. I was never the type to meet a stranger at a bar and go somewhere and have sex. I knew all my partners. I just dated several guys over the next few years.

I mentioned before that I had never participated in drug use, and I didn't. I did not even know anything about drugs. I had heard of Ecstasy because it was the popular drug at all the dance clubs we went to. I knew about weed because there was always weed at the parties we went to. I know that God was watching over me because although I never participated in drug use, there were so many incidents where I could have easily gotten busted and gone to jail, guilty by association. One night I was at a club with some friends, and my best friend at the time was completely wasted. She came up to me and handed me a piece of paper and told me to hold onto it for her. I trusted her. I figured it was some guy's phone number and just put it in my pocket. On the way home later that night, she told me, "Give me my acid!" I told her I didn't know what she was talking about. She started laughing. She was still drunk. She said, "That piece of paper I gave you. It's acid." I almost passed out. I told her to never do anything like that to me again. I could have gotten busted for drugs, and I had never even taken drugs. How was I supposed to know acid, aka LSD, was a paper?

At one point, I quit eating. I lost way too much weight. My mom took me to a counselor. I was being treated for depression. You think? I really did not want to live. But as I mentioned, suicide was out of the question. I was told I would be put in the hospital if I did not start eating. I was terrified of needles. I started eating. What made things even harder was that I would run into that nice guy I dated from time to time at clubs and parties. I felt ashamed every single time I saw him. After all, I had cared for him, and I really did him injustice just to protect my secret. And you know what? He was never mean to me. He was polite when we ran into each other, even if I was with someone else. He was just a good person.

Then one night, I was at a pool hall with some friends. This guy was there. We had a lot of the same friends. I eventually got up the nerve and asked him to go outside with me to talk. I could not take the guilt anymore. Being the sweet person he was, he didn't even ask questions; he just went outside with me. I was trembling and could hardly breathe. I was honest and told him the entire story…the truth of what I did. It was probably especially hard for him since he was an adopted kid. But he listened. I teared up. You could see his heart sink, but at the same time, at least now he had answers to why I left him. He did not look at me with judging eyes, but I knew he was hurt. I asked him to forgive me for not telling him I was pregnant and for everything that took place after I found out I was pregnant. He forgave me and said he wished I would have told him. Then he hugged me. Now that is a good person.

Unfortunately, I could not forgive myself. I kept partying. I kept hanging out with people I should not have been hanging out with. Several of the guys I dated were not high-quality guys. Some were messed up in drugs. Some were poor little rich boys that were bored and would steal stuff just to see if they could get away with it. Some could not stay faithful. One boyfriend showed up at my grandmother's house on Christmas Day and told me to go and get tested for HIV because he had been sharing needles. We both tested. We were both negative for HIV. I lived with one boyfriend in Austin for a while. He was into bodybuilding and was whacked out on steroids one night. He held me down on the couch and choked me. When I broke free and ran outside, he ran after me, tackled me, then dragged me back into our apartment and held me at gunpoint. He even slept in front of the door so I could not leave. It was a townhouse that had only one entry. Then in the morning, he woke up and acted like nothing had happened. That was the end of that, and it needed to be. I was bruised literally and emotionally. I knew I had to get out of that situation.

I did date a couple of "good guys" but managed to mess those relationships up because I didn't think I deserved a good guy. I eventually did something to drive them away. And my "life" wasn't much of one. I went in and out of college. I took some courses at MCC in Waco and ACC in Austin. I kept changing my degree plan. I worked low-paying jobs. I just did not have any focus in life. I was going nowhere good but going there fast. And then one day it happened. I can remember so vividly like it was yesterday. I do not remember where I was when this took place, but I totally recall the experience that led to me taking a different road in life. I was 25 years old at the time, and one day it was like scales fell off my eyes, and I saw my life through God's eyes. And I was disgusted. It was like a movie playing in my head. It was dark, sad, and ugly. I did not feel any condemnation whatsoever. In fact, it was just the opposite. I felt like I had warm arms around me, holding me tight. These arms were full of love and compassion. And as I was seeing all these images of my life and not liking what I saw, I heard God ask me, "What are you doing? I have so much more for you than this." I teared up. I knew exactly what God meant. And I knew immediately what I had to do.

I have always enjoyed reading. And I had recalled reading an article in a Country Music magazine about Trisha Yearwood and Belmont University. Belmont University is in Nashville, Tennessee. The college is very connected to the country music industry. I got in touch with my sister-in-law Jodi, who worked for American Airlines at the time, and asked her to get me a plane ticket to Nashville. I went to Nashville for a couple of days and stayed in the girl's dorm at Belmont. It was summer, and not many girls were in the dorm. I took tours of the campus and was able to ask questions, and I fell in love with Belmont and Nashville.

When I got back to Texas, I told my mom, "I have to get out of here!" I knew I was hanging with people I did not need to be associating with. I was doing stuff I didn't need to be doing. I was too easily influenced. I had to get over my past. I told my mom that I would apply for scholarships and grants and get loans and even sell my car if I had to, but I was moving to Nashville. I applied to Belmont and was ecstatic when I received news that I got in! I remember taking final exams of summer classes at MCC in Waco, Texas, on a Friday and my parents driving me and my belongings to Nashville to start Fall classes at Belmont the following Monday. Whew! I knew there would be no time to look for an apartment, so I signed up to be in the girl's dorm. Yeh, I was probably the only 25-year-old in there, but no one seemed to care. I was just so happy to be there. Time for a new start! I was ready to leave my old life behind and start anew.

"Your past just ended one second ago, so move on!"

-Chuck Swindoll, Pastor, Author, Educator

"The past does not equal the future unless you live there. You are not your behavior. You are not your past… if you're focusing on the past, you'll likely get more of what you've gotten."

-Tony Robbins, Author, Coach, Speaker, Philanthropist

"If you do not change your direction, you may end up where you are heading."

-Lao Tzu, Ancient Chinese Philosopher and Writer

"Walk in the direction of an answered prayer."

-Max Lucado, Pastor at Oak Hills Church in San Antonio, Texas, and Author

"The question isn't, 'are we ever gonna die?' The question is, 'are we ever gonna live?'"

-Erwin McManus, Lead Pastor of Mosaic in Los Angeles, California, and Author, Futurist, Filmmaker

I was ready to LIVE! I felt like so much of my childhood had been taken from me, and I had been forced to grow up way too fast. I viewed moving to Nashville as a gift from God and truly believed something amazing would happen there. There are times in life you may need to take a leap of faith and live with great expectation.

"My Hands Are Open"

-By: Josh Baldwin with Bethel Music

Chapter 5

Letting Go Of Secrets
Finding Hope

I remember my first day in Nashville like it was yesterday. My dad, mom, and I were in the family RV with all the belongings I would need to start a new life. We pulled into the women's dormitory parking lot at Belmont University and proceeded on the adventure to locate my room. When I found my room, there were three girls there: my new roommate Jessi and two of her friends. All three of these young women were tremendously cordial and introduced themselves to my parents and me. I found it amusing that the university paired me, a tall, lanky, Southern girl from Texas, country accent and all, with a short, Italian girl from New York with a strong anything but country accent. But you know what? We hit it off instantly. Jessi had already been at Belmont for a couple of years. Luckily, she already knew everything about Belmont and Nashville. She was able to show me around and give me the lay of the land. In addition, she was a part of the women's softball team at Belmont and therefore was able to introduce me to an entirely new set of friends.

My time at Belmont left me full of wonderful memories. And one little tidbit of information, I was at Belmont as a student the exact same time country music superstar Brad Paisley was there. Brad was a warm and humble individual. He was also extremely sweet. For the Artists and Repertoire class that I took for my minor in Music Business, Brad was gracious and agreed to be the artist that I created a press kit for. I arranged a photoshoot with Brad that turned out to be somewhat of an adventure in itself. My dear friend Shane Tarleton, also a Belmont alumnus, took the pictures. We were poor college students, but luckily Shane was the owner of a very nice camera. Later, I interviewed Brad in order to create a biography on him to complete the press kit. Fun memories.

My years in Nashville had some of the happiest moments in my life up to that point. There are so many wonderful stories that I could share. Maybe in another book. I do believe it is significant that I share specific events that took place while I lived in Nashville. I knew God's hand was completely involved in the process of getting me to Nashville. From me flying out there to spend the weekend to give Belmont a look to actually getting accepted into Belmont and setting up the financial responsibilities and applying for scholarships and grants. Even to the roommate I was matched with, the people I met, and the classes I took. All God. All for a purpose.

As classes began, I would be working towards a Bachelor of Science in Broadcast Communications with that minor in Music Business. Hey, I was in Nashville; I had to do something related to music. Part of the curriculum was a requirement that you had to do internships. You know, working your tail off while not getting paid, but it could be your "foot in the door" into a business opportunity. In truth, the internships were pretty amazing if you got plugged in with the right company. Well, a few weeks into school, I was perusing some of the openings for internships on a billboard in the hallway between classes. I came across one for a Production Assistant for a syndicated show called "Hot, Hip and Country." I called the Producer, and she set up an interview with me. To my surprise, the host of this show was someone I knew. Well, I had seen her on television to a great extent because she was the winner of the 1983 Miss America Pageant, and she was also the host of "TNN Country News" at the time, Debra Maffett.

The Producer for "Hot, Hip and Country," Leah, offered me the internship as the Production Assistant. Yay! Total excitement. I cannot begin to explain to you how completely excited I was. I had not been in Nashville very long, but I had already landed an internship doing what I was going to college for. Score! It had been some time since I had been so totally thrilled about something in my life. I was ready to give 100% to this internship. When the time came for me to go on our first shoot and meet Debra, she was so sweet and kind that it blew me away. I do not know what I was expecting. Here was this woman that I often watched on television, and now we were working together. It was all a bit unreal to me. But I was thrilled.

I was involved with a variety of work for the show. Sometimes I would run camera during interviews or fetch food or pick up Debbie's wardrobe from "Manuel's" or a hundred other little things as needed. Our crew was invited to music video shoots, record release parties, concerts, conferences, and so forth. Debbie would interview country music stars for the show. I could tell you so many stories of how much fun we had and about all the people I was able to meet through this internship. It was a blessing indeed.

Debbie and I became friends during the process of working together. When my internship with "Hot, Hip and Country" was over, Debbie hired me to be her Personal Assistant. I often hung out at her house, and although she was my boss, she was also like my big sister. Debbie was and is a very devout Christian, which is just what I needed in my life at that time. God knew what He was up to.

God used Debbie in all sorts of ways in my life. Debbie was the person that encouraged me to get involved and return to church. She was a wonderful mentor to me. Debbie took the time to share with me many struggles she had gone through and overcome in her own life. She had been Miss America and worked in the Country Music Industry, so I thought, "Her? Problems?" But she had gone through much to get where she was. Her life consisted of stories of pain and heartache. Debbie had become a friend. I trusted her.

With that being said, it came as a total surprise when I was at her house one day, and out of nowhere, as we were talking, she bluntly said to me, "Julie, you are one of the coldest people I have ever met." I think I was a bit flabbergasted. I was like, "What? Me? Cold?" I looked at her and said, "I'm a very nice person!" She responded, "I never said you weren't nice; I said you were cold. You have so many walls built up high around you that no one can even get near you." Ohhhhhhh, that's what she meant. I just sat there for a moment. I wasn't mad. But I wasn't expecting that. I could not deny it, though. It was true. She was right. I think the reason it shocked me is that no one had ever spoken to me like that. Direct, but out of pure love. Debbie had nailed me. I had become an expert at keeping people at arm's length. Most of my life, the people that were supposed to love me the most were the ones that hurt me the most. In response, I just wasn't going to let anyone get close to me again. Ever. The crazy thing is that I did not even know I had been doing that until Debbie pointed it out to me. That was the beginning of many deep, long talks between Debbie and me. I wish I had been journaling back then and had written all our conversations down. My heart remembers the wisdom she spoke into me and the love that she demonstrated to me.

There was another important day with Debbie and me that I would like to share. One day after I had gotten out of classes at Belmont, she called me and asked me what I was doing. I let her know I was free for the afternoon. She asked me to drive out to her house in Brentwood and pick her up and take her to get her car. She had been at a prayer meeting the night before, and she had been too tired to drive home afterward, so she left her car at this house, and a friend drove her home. But now she needed her car. So, I went and picked her up and drove her to the house that the prayer meeting had been at. She asked me if I wanted to go in and meet the family there. I was like, "Not really." I wasn't meaning to be rude. I just wanted to get back to my dorm and lounge. But, in her polite way, Debbie said I would probably enjoy meeting these people. It was just a couple and their teenage son. So, I went in. She knew I would do anything she asked me to. We had not been in the house for three minutes when this man and his son started speaking over me. If someone reading this does not understand the meaning of that, it simply means that they felt like God had shown them some facts about my life, and they, in turn, started praying for me. The more interesting and almost terrifying thing was not only were they speaking over me, but they were also speaking about all the things that had happened in my life as well as the things I had done. I had not told this stuff to anyone but my mom. I felt like I was literally going to pass out. My secrets were no longer secrets. Debbie must have seen the look on my face and came up beside me and held me. At that moment, the wife of this couple came into the room, and all four of them were praying over me. It was Debbie, the couple, and their son. I was asked to forgive those that had done such horrible things to me, and I did. Then I was asked to repent and speak out the name of every man I had ever had sex with. I was like, "Uh, let me think." I don't know what number represents "a lot" of sexual partners, but from the time I was 17 to 25 years of age, I had slept with 13 guys. That seemed like a huge and horrible amount. It made me feel pretty cheap just to speak the number and their names out loud. But I did it. I repented. I forgave them all. At that point, a prayer was spoken over me to break the soul ties that I had made with these men by sleeping with them. I confessed and asked forgiveness for the abortions. I was crying. Debbie was praying fervently. And afterward, I can honestly say I felt like something had lifted off of me. I truly felt like a heavy weight that I had been carrying had been released. I thanked the lovely couple and their son. I knew God had orchestrated this because I had not even told Debbie about the abortions, but these people knew. And God knew I had to let go of the heavy burdens from the previous years of my life. It was a genuine blessing. I will not forget that day.

That was the first time I felt like I was "free" from my past. A substantial part of my past did die that day. Unfortunately, I didn't know it at the time, but it wasn't over. Satan wasn't giving up that easy. Nevertheless, I did feel a bit lighter in spirit. I felt happy. I just felt a little better. This was important because I needed this event to transpire if I was ever going to let people into my life again.

My years at Belmont and in Nashville were the happiest years of my life up until that point. God used Debbie to encourage me to get involved with church activities again, to offer me unconditional love, and assist me in opening up to life once more. My college roommate Jessi played a big part in building a new community of friends around me. These young women showed me what it was like to have good, clean fun. I started laughing more and trusting more. One of my best friends, Shane, taught me how to just let loose, go for it, and have a good time. Shane and I continue to keep in touch. He worked his way up the ladder to a top position at a record label in Nashville. I still love him to death.

The time came when I was required to do another internship for Belmont. I found an opening at TNN. TNN was The Nashville Network. It was a hub for all types of country music programming. I was thrilled when I got the internship at TNN. It was during this time at TNN that I met Dick Clark's son, RAC. He was responsible for establishing a Dick Clark Productions office in Nashville. RAC would oversee operations and production. He and I would chat from time to time. I was amazed that he was Dick Clark's son. I grew up watching American Bandstand, which was hosted by Dick Clark.

One day when I was at my internship, I said to RAC, "Why don't you just give me a job!" And his reply was, "Okay." He was hiring an entire staff and crew for the production of a new talk show. RAC told me he would fit me in somewhere. We discussed how I would work around my last few classes at Belmont. I had just landed a job. Yes! I would just like to mention here that I adamantly do not believe in coincidences at all. I believe every single person I met in Nashville had a purpose in my life.

I loved working for Dick Clark Productions and for RAC. He was an amazing boss. He expected professionalism, but he was also completely laid back, nice and funny. He was a California boy living in the South, and he was vegan. Yeh, we never turned him on to barbecue.

The show that DCP produced was TNN's nighttime one-hour variety country show called "Prime Time Country." It was a busy job but a fun job. Monday through Friday, we would tape shows. We had country artists, actors, and a wide variety of guests, which made work interesting and fun. Daily we had studio rehearsals prior to taping the shows. The show was "live to tape," which meant if something went wrong, the show had to go on. We had no time for editing as the show aired an hour after we taped it. I could go on and on. It was a lot of work, but when you enjoy what you're doing, you don't care.

I made new friends at DCP, and we were one big happy family. We would go out to eat together. Go to sporting events together. We hung out together. Tom Wopat (Luke Duke from "The Dukes of Hazzard) was the show's original host, and he loved to bowl. It was nothing for him to take the entire staff and crew out to eat or bowling after we got through taping shows. Dick Clark himself would fly in from California from time to time, and he would always cater in dinner or provide some other nice gesture for the staff and crew. We always received cool Christmas gifts as well. Dick's philosophy was if you keep your employees happy, they will do great work for you. This is true. Production work can be challenging, and when your boss makes you feel appreciated, you want to give them your very best. It's more than a job. It's family. One time our staff and crew were all flown out to Las Vegas to shoot shows at a theater located in a hotel. The transition from our home studio to working remotely at a theater in Las Vegas had obstacles to overcome, but we got it done. It was hard work but also a great deal of fun. Really great memories.

After some time, I did decide to leave Dick Clark Productions and proceeded to work for TNN's daytime variety show "Crook and Chase." Now Lorianne Crook and Charlie Chase were a hoot to work with. They would do anything we producers asked them to do for a skit. Lorianne's husband Jim had secured a theater in Myrtle Beach one summer, and the staff all moved out there temporarily. We stayed in timeshare homes provided for us. One sunny summer afternoon, we had Lorianne visit a wildlife preserve and take part in bathing with an elephant in a pond as part of a skit. Lorianne was in scuba-type clothing and rode on the back of the elephant into the water for bath time. The following day, that same elephant was brought to the theater and walked onstage during the taping of the show. As soon as the elephant was brought in, it took its trunk and cupped Lorianne's breast. Charlie had to walk off stage because he was laughing so hard. Lorianne's eyes just got extremely big. The entire staff and crew, me included, were hysterical with laughter. But we could not stop taping. The elephant caretaker immediately addressed the issue. The caretaker then expressed to Lorianne and everyone watching that elephants are very smart. The elephant had remembered that Lorianne had bathed with him the previous day and what the elephant had done with his trunk was actually a sign of affection. This may not have been the best story to share, but I just adored the fact that Crook and Chase were so adventurous and would do whatever we asked them to do. "Crook & Chase" was another absolutely fun job. Brad Paisley was also a guest when we were out in Myrtle Beach, and yes, I produced that segment. It was good to see him again.

I enjoyed the internships and the jobs I was able to work within the country music television industry. During those years, I still had time to build a strong bond with several friends inside and outside of church. For a while, I went to a small startup church with Debbie. As time went on, my friend Ana invited me to her church. Debbie understood that I needed to be in a church that had people my age in it. Ana took me to Christ Church in Brentwood, Tennessee, and to her "20-30-year-olds" Sunday school class. This is where I really started pressing into my faith again. I made so many friends. We established a supper club and would have potluck get-togethers monthly. Pastor Hardwick and Pastor Stan at Christ Church were huge parts in getting me interested in church and God again. I, without a doubt, experienced much healing in some areas of my life during my time in Nashville. Subsequently, I truly thought I was 100% better. I hardly dated during my years in Nashville. I went out with one guy several times and another guy one time. Then I told God that dating really wasn't my thing. I decided I did not want to date anyone further until God had my future husband ready for me to meet.

I did graduate from Belmont with honors. I must be honest. I was stunned during college graduation rehearsal when I was given a yellow tassel to wear around my neck. I asked, "What's this?" I was told I was graduating

Cum Laude, and I was to wear the tassel around my neck during graduation. I could not believe it. For the girl who struggled through high school to then graduate from college with honors, I was truly thankful.

Over time if I remember correctly, CBS had bought out TNN, then Viacom bought out CBS and eventually canceled all of the country music programming. "Crook & Chase" was the last show to be canceled. I remember our very last taping. Garth Brooks was one of our guests. I have to admit, I had taken several pictures with Garth over the years. He was my favorite…so sweet and down to earth. "Crook & Chase" taped the last show and packed up. There were hundreds of television people without jobs at that point. I considered looking for jobs in other fields of work, but I went to college for television, and I loved it. Some friends moved off to California. Some to other states. All I knew other than Nashville was Texas, so I decided to move home. The idea of leaving Nashville was hard. Real hard. I had found stability there. I had experienced some healing there. I had found hope there. I had reconnected with God and church. I had made so many amazing friends. I had begun to live again.

I called my parents and asked them if I could move back into their house until I found a job. Since my job at "Crook and Chase" ended due to cancelation and I wasn't fired, I was able to collect unemployment for a time. After I said my goodbyes in Nashville and moved back to Texas, I began the hunt for a new job and new life again. Every Sunday, I would drive into town and buy the newspapers from Dallas, Fort Worth, Austin, San Antonio, and Houston in order to look for job postings. Yes, this was before social media and job sites, and we still had to look in newspapers for job ads. Unfortunately, there just were hardly any television jobs. I concluded that I had to look into other fields of work whether I liked it or not. Two weeks before my unemployment was to run out, and after sending out countless resumes, I saw a television job in the newspaper. I immediately sent my resume' and received the call for an interview. This particular job would be working for a Christian talk show. The interview went well. In the end, I was hired as an Associate Producer and moved to the Dallas-Fort Worth Metroplex.

I had experienced so much healing, friendships, encouragement, a church, home, and hope in Nashville. I would not know until years later what moving back to Texas would do to me subconsciously. But I had a new job, I found an apartment, and I had to hit the ground running.

Let us take a moment to talk about secrets. I know that we all have personal lives, and I believe that we have the right to protect our privacy. That is not what I am talking about when referring to secrets. I had secrets. Better yet, deep secrets had me. And they were tearing me apart because I was always wondering what would happen if people found out my secrets. There are times we need to talk about our secrets in order to keep them from destroying us. I had no intention of exposing my secrets, so God revealed them in a safe place, surrounded by love, so I would have to face the secrets. Once this happened, I could breathe a little easier. I wasn't judged. I found a little strength. I found hope. I realized I wasn't the "bad person" I thought I was. The Bible has this to say about secrets:

"For everything that is hidden will eventually be brought into the open, and every secret will be brought to light."

-Mark 4:22 (NLT)

I have heard this scripture quoted in reference to different circumstances, but for my life, my secrets had to be uncovered, and I had to face them. It was the best-case scenario for me. I also had a trusted friend, Debbie, who was there to walk through this time and what I was going through with me. Please do not tell your secrets to just anyone. I have read things on social media that have astounded me. Social media is not the place for your secrets. Later, when I discuss the trauma therapy I went through, you may decide therapy is for you. Maybe not. My point here is that if you are holding onto a secret that is causing great pain, insecurity, depression, or anxiety in your life, it may be time to share that secret. It should not control your life. I am not a doctor. I just know what secrets did in my life and how my life turned toward betterment when what was hidden was brought to the light. Pray about your situation and ask God what you should do. My prayer for you is that you find hope. Hope is found in letting go of the secrets, the past, which makes this song fitting:

"Burn The Ships"

-By: for King & Country

Recently, Joyce Meyer was in the studio with us to tape shows. She was promoting her latest book "Authentically, Uniquely You." I knew some of Joyce's life story, but I did not realize that as a child, she was the victim of incest at the hands of her father. Our host, Sheila Walsh, asked Joyce whether it was harder to forgive her father or her mother. Joyce was honest and replied that it was, in fact, harder to forgive her mother because her mother knew it was happening and did nothing about it. Joyce explained how her childhood affected her adult life in so many negative ways. She shares her story in hopes of helping others deal with trauma from their pasts. Sheila went on to ask Joyce what advice she would give people regarding failure because so many people today feel like failures. Here is Joyce Meyer's reply, and I hope it shines light into something you may see as a dark shadow in your life:

"We can fail forward. In fact, I don't think you can succeed without failing. Because I've learned so much by the things I've done wrong."

-Joyce Meyer, Author, Speaker

Hope is everywhere if you just look for it. Failure cannot overtake your destiny in life. Secrets cannot keep you in a dark place unless you allow them to. You are worth so much more. Believe it.

Chapter 6

Marriage And Missteps
Understanding Where Each Of Us Comes From

I began my new job in June of 2000. I was excited to work for a Christian talk show and felt the spiritual environment would affect me in a positive way. I always laugh when I recall my first day. Believe it or not, I got sent home to change clothes. I had on a business suit which consisted of a jacket and pencil skirt, and my knees were slightly showing. I was not aware of the dress code because it was my first day. Nevertheless, if a woman wore a dress or skirt, her knees could not show. Leave it to me to break the rules on the first day. I am just having fun. I did not get in trouble. I just had to go home and change.

In Nashville, my jobs were more on the creative side. I helped book talent, made sure contracts were signed, pitched segment ideas, wrote scripts, conceptualized skits, and so forth. At this new job, I would be producing and editing a daily show. The previous television shows that I worked for were not edited because the shows went up to satellite an hour after we taped them. With my new position, shows were taped about six weeks in advance of airing. Therefore, after taping, I would, and still do, cut the raw footage of the shows together in order to prepare them to air. The other Associate Producer, Zabrina, was amazing. She was patient and diligent and taught me everything I needed to know with this new job.

Approximately a month after I started this new adventure, another new hire came on board. He was an editor named David Butler. I was assigned to work with David to prepare shows to be aired on television. Every Monday morning, there would be a production meeting and prayer time with the production staff. This was a wonderful way to really get to know my co-workers. David and I began to talk daily because we had to work together as a team. Not only was he a production editor, David was also a youth pastor at the church he had been attending since he was 9 years old. As David and I got to know each other, I found out he had been married since he was 19. Now I want to point out that I had absolutely nothing to do with his divorce. Remember, I had told God that I did not want to date until I met my future husband, and I had not dated at all in almost two years. David was married, and I was not interested in him or anyone. I was still adjusting to moving to a new city and learning a new job.

Little did anyone know, but David's marriage was already heading for divorce. And by the end of 2000, he and his wife were separating. His soon-to-be ex-wife moved back up North with her family, and David moved back in with his parents as he began to sort out his life. David's divorce went swiftly. He slowly began communicating what he was going through to some people that he worked closely with. That would include me since we worked together. I felt sorry for him, but I did not know what led to the divorce. I didn't know his ex and barely knew him; therefore, work went on as usual.

David and I did start to talk more and became friends. He eventually asked me out, and I was very honest and said no because we were good friends by now, and I wasn't interested in him in that way. I had not said what I said to be mean; I just didn't think we would "work out." I did not want either of us to start dating then possibly end up getting hurt. Also, we worked together. What if we bombed and then still had to see each other every day at work? How uncomfortable would that be? But David was persistent. I remembered asking God not to let any man be interested in me or ask me out until it was my future husband. David asked, and we did indeed go out.

The courtship was fast and furious. He wanted to keep our dating secret because he did not know how it would be viewed for him to be dating so soon after his divorce. After all, he was a pastor. No one at work knew we were dating. His family did not know. His Senior Pastor and his church did not know either. It felt strange keeping us a secret. One afternoon, David and I went out for lunch, and other people from work showed up at the same restaurant. We freaked out. They just waved, and nothing was said. It was probably just assumed that we were co-workers enjoying a break from the office together.

When David and I eventually did go public with our relationship, the news was received well by some people. On the other hand, certain individuals did not receive the announcement well at all. David had several people tell him our relationship was a mistake and that I was just a "re-bound" due to the fact he had been in a marriage that ended in divorce. Some individuals told him he needed to take more time and date around, make sure he was totally healed from his first marriage, and so forth. Wow! This did not exactly make me feel great. I was already very nervous or just felt weird dating a pastor. During my time in Nashville, I had come a long way in dealing with my past, but I will be entirely honest and admit that I was wondering if God was playing some kind of joke. I was waiting to see if the other shoe would fall. Me? Marry a pastor? Did God remember how messed up my life had been? I did come clean with David and told him everything about my past because he deserved to know. I wanted him to make an informed decision about whether he really wanted to be with someone that had gone through the things I went through. David was fine with it. His thought process on it all was that we all have a past, we all make mistakes, no one is perfect, and he had his own share of things he didn't want the world to know about, so we were good. I wish it would have been that simple.

Meeting David's family was interesting. We met for lunch one afternoon at a local restaurant. I was to meet David's parents, sister, niece, and nephew. I adored David's dad, Tom, immediately. Tom was a former military person. He had been in Army intelligence. Tom had a very dry sense of humor and was naturally funny. I never questioned how much Tom loved me. He treated me wonderfully from day one. I had great honor and respect for Tom. He made me and everyone laugh constantly. You could not be around Tom and not laugh. David's mom, Joyce, on the other hand, did not think that highly of me. She grew to love me over the years, but she never really "liked" me. I don't know if that will make sense to everyone reading this. The best way I can explain it is that Joyce was cordial towards me and treated me nicely, but I was a Baptist girl and not a Pentecostal girl like she had wanted for her son David. This fact will come into our story again later. I do not want you to think I am being disrespectful regarding Joyce. I just need you to realize that her dislike for me caused many problems in my and David's marriage over the years. Many problems.

Joyce was friendly towards me most of the time, but she was also very opinionated and had no problem saying what was on her mind. Joyce and I had a few escalated conversations over the years. These exchanges between us usually had to do with my lack of interest in serving in ministry and how David and I were raising our children. What I am doing here is trying to establish the issues that were taking place within David and my marriage.

In the time that I have participated in therapy with my psychologist, I have learned that there are "building blocks" in our lives that contribute to the way we see ourselves, the way we think, and even affect our actions and the way we respond to situations and words spoken to us. Individuals telling David I was a "re-bound" and that he should not marry me as well as my relationship with David's mother were building blocks that were establishing negative thought processes as well as stirring up old thought processes that I thought I had overcome. Just as a spider spins an intricate, delicate web, we cannot forget that the web is used for the capture, struggle, and death of the spider's prey. A web of tangled emotions began to build in my mind, and I did not even know it. There could be words that had been spoken to you 20 years ago that are negatively affecting your life today. Or an incident that seemed like no big deal may have lodged in your subconscious and contributed to many wrong decisions over the span of your life. Trauma does not have to be physical abuse, a car accident, a parent leaving, or something we might term as a major event. Trauma can be something seemingly simplistic. But it's like the spider web; it can take your life if you can't pull away from it. The enemy sets the trap, and we don't even see what's coming.

David had been at the same church since he was 9 years old, as I previously mentioned. His home church was referred to as a non-denominational church, but it was basically a Pentecostal church except we could wear make-up, pants, and cut our hair, and so forth. The Senior Pastor and his wife were like second parents to David. They had never had children of their own and looked at David as a son. When David felt called to preach at the age of 12, his pastor took him under his wings and started training David for ministry. David became the Youth Pastor at his church when he was still just a teenager himself. Once David and I were engaged, he wanted to go to his pastor and wife for pre-marital counseling.

David had been married before. I had not. But I had decided that I would "do things right" this time. I did not have a choice when I was 17, but I did now. I had not dated in two years prior to David and had no problem telling him we were going to wait until our wedding night to be together. In my heart, I truly felt as though doing things the "proper" Christian way would make everything different this time, and our relationship would be blessed. Why do I even bring that up? In order to demonstrate that we all have the power to make the right decisions and I needed this to be my decision to wait.

Back to pre-marital counseling. All I really want to say in regard to this subject is that I believe pre-marital counseling is a good thing, a needed thing. Whether you have been married before or not, you might want to consider it. The process allows you to lay everything out on the table, open for discussion. Retrospectively due to some conversations that had been held in private with David, I do not believe his pastor and wife were at all happy about David getting married again so soon. Even so, they were nice to me. The main thing I want to point out here is that I felt led to make something abundantly clear during counseling. I detected that I needed to make the statement, "I do not feel called to ministry. I will be a support to David and help him to thrive in ministry in any way that I can, but I am marrying David. I am not marrying this church."

Now, some people may think I was being rude or mean. I can assure you that I was not. My intention was just the opposite. My past had taught me that keeping secrets and not being upfront and honest could lead to disaster, and I did not want any unrealistic expectations placed on me. I will do whatever I feel God calls me to do. But I do not want expectations of others to be placed on me to do something that I do not feel gifted to do.

My honesty seemed to be received well, and I was told that being a helpmate to David was all that I needed to be. Years later, I found out, from David, that the agreement regarding any role I might or might not have in the church wasn't really received as well as we had thought. In all reality, there were multiple people in the church who were not happy that I was not serving in ministry in some capacity. Of course, David and I did not find this out until years later.

Why do I tell you all of this? Am I trying to get you to feel sorry for me? No. Is it to paint a negative picture of other people that were a part of David and my marriage? No. Every detail I am sharing with you is to build a background of what led to the eventual breaking point and emotional collapse I experienced. Throughout David and my 17-year marriage, there were individuals in David's family and in our church that made life very difficult between us. And if anyone reading this has ever been in a similar situation, you know how hard it is to paint on a smile and act like all is well around people you know do not think highly of you. It is hard…especially when you haven't even done anything wrong. You are disliked for just being you. You don't live up to the expectations of others. You're not good enough. There's something wrong with you. Remember the quote I shared with you earlier:

"Guilt tells us we've done something wrong. Shame tells us we are something wrong."

--Sheila Walsh, Author, Speaker, Television Host

I did not know it at the time, but all those little voices in my head that had been buried in my subconscious that I thought had been healed were being awakened again. I was being shamed for just being me. I now know that these events, shall we say, opened an old can of worms. When you are not fully healed from trauma in your life, even when you have experienced great breakthroughs, your mind and emotions are ready to unlock a destructive force that can make you relapse into total brokenness. No matter how strong you may have become, when you have multiple people making you question your own worth, it is just a waiting game as to when emotional overload, and the enemy, take you down.

Joyce thought it was ridiculous that David and I were having a wedding. After all, he already had a wedding once before. David had to tell his mom, "Yeh, but Julie hasn't." I was thirty-one and "finally" was getting married. My dad's nickname for me was "old maid." My brothers had gotten married when they were young in life. My dad had wondered if marriage would ever happen for me. Dad had no problem voicing his opinion on that subject. Therefore, when David and I got engaged, I thought dad would be happy. I think he was indeed delighted for us. Even so, I did not know if my dad would even come to my wedding. Odd thought from me? Not really.

When I was in high school, it was customary that if you were nominated for Homecoming Queen, your father would escort you onto the football field. My dad did not, and still does not, like crowds, so he refused to be my escort. I was the only girl out there without her daddy. That may not seem like a big deal. But it was. When all the other homecoming princesses were latched onto their dad's arm as they strolled onto the field, I was the odd girl out. My brother Vance was off the hard drugs at this point and agreed to walk me out onto the football field. Homecoming wasn't a total embarrassment. At least I was not out on the field alone.

In the end, my dad agreed to walk me down the aisle for my wedding but not before he made my mom promise to burn the suit afterward and not bury him in anything other than his work clothes. My dad is a farmer and proud of it. He is not into fancy things like suits. But he wore one to give me away at my wedding, and he looked quite nice, I must say.

I want to take a moment here. Regardless of what I have shared in this chapter, I want you to know that in spite of my differences with Joyce, I could never thank her enough. She took early retirement after David and I had Sofia. David and I both had to work; we were a two-income family. Joyce did not want to witness us putting Sofia in daycare, so she retired early to watch Sofia for us. I am not saying that anything is wrong with putting a child in daycare. David and I eventually had to put Sofia and Lily in daycare years later. But Sofia had special needs as an infant that you will learn of in a later chapter. Joyce wanted to make sure Sofia was cared for properly. Joyce may have had her issues with me, but she loved and adored our children, so for that alone, she was an amazing human being and a wonderful grandmother to Sofia and Lily.

Additionally, I will say that everyone has a story, and so did Joyce. She had a challenging childhood that I do not honestly believe she ever recovered from. Joyce shared many stories from her childhood. She experienced trauma as well, although I don't believe she recognized it as trauma. And hurt people hurt people.

On the other hand, as for our pastor and his wife, they just believed differently than me in some areas, so I never lived up to their expectations. I was aware of this, and this caused issues in my marriage and even within me. Even so, to this day, our children still call them Papaw and Mimi since they consider David their son.

Furthermore, as for my dad, he is a great man. He turned 80 recently and still farms. My dad showed me what an exceptional work ethic looks like. He was an excellent provider for our family. He has never been a social person, and he does not like to be around crowds. That's just who he is. We now have a great relationship, and he is my dad, and I love him. I realize now, though, that many of these events and situations that took place over the years had a very damaging impact on me. I needed a daddy to be present in my life and to make me feel special. And the expectations of others slowly made me start questioning my worth again as well as making me a little angry inside.

David and I did get married on March 9, 2002. There were probably some "red flags" we should have noted and discussed deeply, but we got married because it was what we wanted to do. It was a small wedding. I had not really had time to make new friends since I had moved back to Texas. I started a new job, found a church, visited my family almost every weekend since they were only two hours away, and eventually started dating David. There were a couple of ladies at work that I had budding friendships with but no close friendships yet. Needless to say, I was beyond excited when my three best friends from Nashville all agreed to come to Texas to serve as my bridesmaids. I was completely overjoyed that they would be a part of my special day. A girl dreams of her wedding most of her life. It was a happy day. I felt beautiful. David looked handsome. We didn't have a care in the world. My best friend caught the bouquet. David and I drove away in my SUV, listening to Will Smith. True story. Unfortunately, David and I started having issues in our marriage almost immediately after we said, "I do."

Before I go any further, I have already told you so much about the experiences I went through up until this point in my life. I think it is very important to mention that David had gone through some hard situations as well. He was not physically abused in any way. He was not involved in drugs or alcohol. But he was raised in a very legalistic surrounding. There were some controlling people in his life. He was not really allowed to be a kid. He wanted to play football but wasn't allowed to. He was at church every time the doors were open. Church is not a bad thing. Church is one of my favorite places to be. But David needed so much more than what he lived in his childhood. His first marriage was one trial after another, from what I have been told. He made some mistakes in his younger years, just as I did. He also made some wrong choices, just as I did. I realize what I am saying here is immensely vague, but I want to protect his privacy in this area. The only point to me saying any of this at all is to say that two broken people like David and myself were a recipe for disaster, and we didn't even know it.

Chapter 7

Where Infertility And A Birth Defect Were The Problems
God Already Had The Answers

If any person reading this, female or male, has ever or is suffering through fertility issues, I will take a moment here to pray for you. I can remember when I was a child and found out how babies were made, I was absolutely grossed out. I recall adamantly telling my mother that I was never getting married or having babies. Not me. No way. Yeh, that changed obviously. Before I even graduated high school, I had told my mom that I had every intention of adopting a little Asian girl someday. Where did that come from? I didn't know. But God knew.

Once I embraced the idea of becoming a mom, the thought filled me with great joy. Great expectation. I was going to be the best mom in the world! I was going to be nurturing. I was going to be fun and adventurous. I was going to be the cool mom. But most of all, I was going to be the mom that affirmed my children and loved them beyond measure. When David and I initiated the discussion regarding children, we made the decision that five children sounded like a good amount. Yes, I said five. I was already in my 30s; therefore, there was no time to waste. David and I were not getting pregnant, though. Surely there wasn't something "wrong" with one of us. Right? Normally if there is an unexpected setback, the issue tends to be with the woman. It seemed most logical that I was the first to get evaluated. Was something not working correctly in my female anatomy? Would I be able to get pregnant?

David and I were relieved to discover that everything was working as it should within my body. We then turned our focus to locating a male fertility doctor for David. We did indeed find an amazing doctor for David. The doctor discovered that David was not producing semen for some unknown reason. Needless to say, the following year or so was not the greatest for us but especially for David. Life became a continual routine of doctor visits, specimen samples, medications, and lab tests. Then came an unexpected and painful surgery where David had to be cut open where no man should ever have to get cut open. This procedure was performed in order to see if there was a varicocele issue. What this specifically means is that if a man has a varicocele issue, this could lead to low sperm production and decreased sperm quality, which can cause infertility. There is your medical lesson for the day. At the conclusion of all that had been attempted, the doctor said that David was sterile and could not have children. The doctor added that we should consider getting pregnant using donor sperm.

David was so beside himself. This was an ache that he never could prepare for. He was a youth pastor. He adored kids. He had always wanted to be a dad. Neither one of us could believe this was happening. We had fasted and prayed and believed David would be able to have children. But in that moment, he was understandably angry. When the doctor suggested a donor, David was adamantly against it. His exact words were, "That's like sending in the second-string quarterback to do what the main guy couldn't get done!" I was devastated.

The doctor had to step up to David to put it kindly. This doctor had seen this exact situation play out many times before with other patients. He basically told David that this predicament sucked, and he hated it for David and me, but that David should not take away my opportunity to have a child because there was absolutely nothing wrong with me. The doctor also told David that there was one last "Hail Mary" procedure that he could try. He also suggested that David and I have donor sperm on standby in the event the procedure was not successful.

David was still against the idea of us using a donor. He could not stand the idea of me being pregnant by another man. At this point, God stepped in. David told me about this encounter later. Basically, David was in one of our spare bedrooms yelling at God one day. David was understandably upset, and he needed to get it off his chest. Why was this happening to him? To us? He had a heart for children. He wanted to be a dad. David was mad. Mad at God. Mad in general. At the conclusion of David's tirade, he said that God asked him, "Was Joseph the biological father of Jesus?" David answered, "No." Then God added, "But look what a difference Joseph made in the life of Jesus, and he raised Jesus as his own child." At that point, David said he could not really argue anymore. He was ready to proceed using donor sperm if necessary. We were both still praying for a miracle of healing for David at the same time as we moved one step closer to pregnancy.

I undertook the responsibility of researching and finding a fertility doctor for myself. I was fully examined again. My amazing doctor suggested David and I utilize a cryobank that had impeccable ethics. He suggested one that he had patients use, and shortly thereafter, David and I received a catalog from California Cryobank. Yes, a catalog of sperm donors. Quite frankly, that was not really anything I thought I would ever be required to do. Purchase sperm. Yeh, awkward but also interesting.

David and I both looked through the catalog at length. We wanted to find a donor that matched a lot of David's physical attributes. We found a few that were around David's height, same eye color, curly to wavy brown hair, and so forth. After much analysis and discussions, we decided on the donor that we wanted to acquire sperm from. My doctor placed the order for a vial of sperm from the donor David and I had chosen. My fertility doctor would retain the vial in the case that we needed to use it.

Specifically, I want to point out the magnitude of what we were up against. David and I were given a 9% to 12% chance of getting pregnant. The factor for this low possibility was that I was 35, and this would be considered an "elderly pregnancy." Yes, those were the exact words that were used to describe me getting pregnant. But we were all in! Odds had nothing on us. We had God on our side and forged forward with every ounce of hope and faith that we could muster. David and I were also still believing for success in the final procedure that David would endure. We told ourselves the donor sperm was just a precaution.

If you are a woman and have ever gone through in-vitro fertilization, God bless you. You are made of grit, determination, and just plain inner strength. I had absolutely no clue as to what my body was about to be put through. I was willing and anxious to do whatever it took to get pregnant. Adding to our family and becoming parents were dreams for David and me. Alas, I remember the day that the sizeable box was delivered to our front door containing all the medications and needles. Lots and lots of needles. I began crying. I had always been terrified of shots, and this was going to require numerous shots. Numerous, in my upper thigh, in my belly, in my hip. Saying I was overwhelmed when this box came to us in the mail would be an understatement. I was scared, but my desire to be a mom was bigger than my fear. I was ready to get this thing started.

A wonderful nurse taught David how to administer shots by using an orange to replicate my skin. This was necessary since I would be receiving multiple shots every single day. David became an expert at administering shots. I trusted his steady hand, and he never hurt me…even when David had to find an area that was not bruised from all the injections.

Weeks passed, which seemed like months, of daily shots. Then the time came for my eggs to be retrieved. I remember that day intensely. David and I had to be at separate hospitals for each of our procedures. Our pastor and his wife would be taking David to see his doctor. The procedure David would endure involved being cut open and scraped in order to see if there were any possible viable sperm that could be used to fertilize my eggs. David would then be driven to the hospital I was checked into in order to have the specimen tested. This may not be the appropriate time to mention this, but my former father-in-law oversaw being my caretaker for the day. Remember how I told you that Tom had an amazing sense of humor? Well, when he requested the day off work, his boss, in turn, asked why Tom needed the day off. Tom's reply was, "I have to go and get my daughter-in-law pregnant." His boss didn't ask any more questions. Tom told the truth. Sort of. Always the jokester.

I recall waking up in my recovery room. My doctor had retrieved my eggs. I was groggy and nauseous and about to throw up. Just so you will know, I am allergic to anesthesia. Every single time I have been put under for a surgical procedure, I wake up throwing up. Not pleasant. Although I was not aware, David had been brought to the hospital where I was a patient. Once the act of throwing up had taken place, I heard talking outside of my room. What I heard broke my heart. It was my doctor. He sadly explained to David that the specimen that had been retrieved that morning had no traces of sperm. The doctor needed final approval from David to use the donor sperm in order to inseminate my eggs. I heard David give his approval.

The following weeks were agonizing and exciting all at once. Our lives were an emotional roller coaster, most certainly. David and I were given daily updates on how many eggs were growing and how many were dying. In-vitro fertilization is a very intricate process. The day came that we were asked to come back to the hospital. David and I only had two surviving eggs left. The other cells had failed to divide and grow. As a result, they died off. David and I decided to implant the two surviving eggs. The waiting began.

When the day arrived that David and I were to go to my doctor's office for a pregnancy test, we were holding hands, excited yet trembling. We trusted God. We had done everything we possibly could for this procedure to be successful. Still, there are no guarantees of a resulting pregnancy when going through in-vitro fertilization.

I was tested. David and I sat in the doctor's office, waiting, praying, hoping, believing. As the nurse came around the corner to where David and I were seated, she asked if we wanted to know the results right then or have the results sent to us. Really? Is that even a consideration? We were like, "Please just tell us now!" The nurse smiled and uttered the words we had been longing to hear, "You're pregnant!" YES! YES! YES! Amen! We started thanking God right there in the middle of that office. We were having a baby!

Now, remember in the story of Job from the Bible, God redeemed everything that had been taken from Job. Without a doubt, I believed that this pregnancy represented the beginning of God redeeming events that had taken place in my life. Why? Well, my first abortion had taken place in December. Our due date for this pregnancy was December 25.

I want to interject some facts at this point in an effort for you to continue to follow my emotional state of mind. When David and I were initially trying to get pregnant, and nothing was happening, the enemy had a party in my head. Trust me when I tell you I was bombarded with thoughts of how I had been pregnant twice before but chose to terminate those pregnancies. This was payback. I didn't deserve to be a mom. To add to our heartache, a well-meaning married couple told David and me that our faith must be lacking; otherwise, we would have gotten pregnant the old fashion way. Another person suggested that David and I must not have prayed enough; otherwise, God would have healed David, and we would not be going through all of the issues that were upon us.

Please allow me to make a suggestion. When couples are already going through the heart-breaking reality of infertility, the last thing they need to hear is that their faith is questionable. Couples who are experiencing infertility need support, not accusations. I know these people probably meant well, but their words were overwhelmingly hurtful.

I was so very careful throughout my pregnancy. I ate meticulously well. I avoided caffeine altogether. I took my prenatal supplements. I never missed a routine doctor visit. I read numerous books on pregnancy. I undertook light exercise. I wanted to do everything right in order for David and me to have a successful pregnancy. As my tummy grew, David would talk to our baby every night before I went to sleep.

With the fact that I was older, we were asked to do a sonogram to see if our baby had any birth defects or issues that needed to be addressed. The sonogram went well, but we were then asked to do an amniocentesis to see if our baby had Down's Syndrome. There is a risk with amniocentesis that it could cause a miscarriage. We told the doctor that we had no interest in such a test and that if our child had Down's, we would not love him or her any less. David and I were then asked if we wanted to know the sex of our baby, and without hesitation, we replied together, "YES!" We found out we would be having a little girl. A sweet, precious little girl. David teared up and said, "I'm sunk!" A little girl was going to have David wrapped around her little finger, and he knew it. It was such a sweet moment. It was beautiful.

David and I enjoyed the moment and then immediately grabbed our phones to share the news with everyone who was anxiously waiting to hear from us. We could not contain our excitement. Our family and friends shared in our excitement. David and I had culminated a long list of possible names that we were considering regarding our baby. We had narrowed down the list, then decided to name our little girl Sofia Analiese. Sofia means "Wisdom," and Analiese has two meanings which are "Consecrated to God" and "Graced with God's bounty." That's our girl! We wanted her name to mean something, and we were quite taken with what these names represented.

The pregnancy went remarkably well. The only issue I dealt with was motion sickness. I had decided to purchase Sea-Bands which apply acupressure buttons on your wrists and are an effective, non-invasive, safe treatment for nausea and vomiting. The bands worked like a charm. Thank God because I could not have ridden in a car otherwise.

Being first-time parents, David and I had no idea that if you wanted to have pictures taken of your baby while you are pregnant, you should do that earlier than the 8-month mark. But I scheduled the appointment. David and I wanted to get a look at Sofia and get a picture of her inside my belly. The lady performing the sonogram was having problems getting a good picture of Sofia. We finally asked what the problem was, and she showed us a picture and told us, "Her feet are in front of her face." We just looked at her. The lady added, "Her feet should not be covering her face." David and I must have looked confused. She then told us that she did not want to alarm us, but she thought there was a problem with our baby. She added that she really believed that Sofia was breech and that we should probably contact our doctor. David and I were a little freaked out. Okay, we were a lot freaked out. We got in our vehicle and began praying. We did not believe God had brought us this far just to have something go wrong.

When David and I were able to get in to see my OB-GYN, she examined me and said that she could feel the head and that everything seemed well. I looked at David then asked my doctor, "Are you sure it's her head you are feeling?" My doctor looked puzzled then asked why I would ask such a question. We proceeded to tell her what had happened when we tried to get a picture of Sofia. In response, my doctor just said, "Well, if it will make you feel better, I can do an ultrasound." David and I both replied, "Yes, please."

The doctor put the cold gel on my belly and began to look at Sofia. By the look on my doctor's face, we could tell something was not right. She cleaned me off and had me sit up. In truth, Sofia was indeed breech, and she had evidently been that way for some time. David and I were told there was no hope of turning Sofia because her little bottom was so stuck in the birth canal that any attempt would most likely hurt her. In addition, I was running low on amniotic fluid, so there was a chance of Sofia going into shock. My doctor instructed us to proceed to the hospital immediately. She suggested we go and take care of all the paperwork in administration, then go home and rest because we would be at the hospital the following morning to have a baby. Sofia would be about three weeks early, but there was no concern for that. A C-section? I was excited to meet Sofia sooner but a bit scared as well.

David and I called our families and close friends. We also had to let work know we would not be back for several weeks. On December 6, 2005,

David and I went to the hospital to have our Sofia. Family members and friends were present. I think I was nervous about the epidural more than anything, but my doctor was an expert, and I did not feel a thing. Literally, I did not feel a thing. After administering the epidural, the doctor told me to put my legs up on the table. I responded to him that I could not even feel my legs, much less lift them. It was a funny moment that I needed at the time.

The incision was commencing when I asked, "Where's my husband? Can someone please get him?" By the time David arrived in the operating room, the doctors were just pulling the amniotic sac out of my belly. You heard Sofia start screaming immediately. Her cries were music to my ears. Our baby girl had arrived. Sofia cried and cried as they were cleaning her up. Remember I mentioned that David would talk to Sofia every night while she was in my belly? Well, she was screaming upon her arrival, so David went over and started talking to her. Sofia immediately stopped crying. She knew her dad's voice.

Looking back on the video David captured in the delivery room was both sad and kind of funny. Sofia had been breech for so long, which resulted in her legs popping back up every time the nurse would try to put her legs down to wrap and swaddle her. Sofia would be, "Folded up like a taco," David would say. As we were getting our first glimpse of Sofia, her poor little genital area was black and bruised from being stuck in the birth canal. The nurses eventually had Sofia's legs straightened out, and they quickly wrapped her up.

Sofia was placed in my arms. Here she was. She was so tiny. So beautiful. So perfect. Everything was there. She was breathing. It is a moment I will never forget. I am sure all moms know exactly what I am talking about. I didn't want that moment to end. I just kept staring at this precious tiny miracle.

Once I was taken into a room, and everyone was getting their turn holding Sofia, my eyes met Tom's, and he saw it coming. He had witnessed this previously when my eggs were extracted. I started throwing up all over the place. When you throw up, your core tightens. When you just went through a C-Section, and your core tightens, well, I yelled loud enough in sheer pain that I am sure several floors in that hospital heard me. Things went downhill for me health-wise at that point.

Again, being first-time parents, David and I weren't the most informed on parenting responsibilities. We had thought we still had plenty of time to find a pediatrician. We were wrong. Here is another instance where God showed up big in light of the lack of David's and my parenting skills. It had been a long, priceless, tiring, and glorious day. It was late, and everyone had left. I was in constant pain, but the saying is true. I knew what moms meant when they said they would go through all the pain again for the sake of their children. I understood what they meant. A nurse entered my room and told David and me that the pediatrician on call had examined Sofia, and there was an issue. We tried to be optimistic, but after infertility, medications, surgeries, complications, and all that accompanied these issues, our minds went straight to the thought, "Here we go again." Dr. David Granger had discovered that because Sofia had been breech for so long, her hip sockets had never been able to form. David and I were a bit perplexed. Basically, with the absence of hip sockets, Sofia's femur bones had no connection to the upper half of her body. What? We had never heard of any such thing like that in our lives. It did not even seem possible. How could this be happening? How would we fix this? What now? Dr. Granger was beyond calming and informative. Even so, David and I were in shock. Not our Sofia! David and I made an appointment to see Dr. Granger the day after I was released from the hospital. For the most part, other than being slightly premature, Sofia was healthy. But her body was not. Dr. Granger referred us to Scottish Rite Hospital for Sofia's treatment.

David and I were beside ourselves. We did not know what to think. We were more than a bit stunned. We were scared for our newborn, Sofia. We did what we always do; we prayed. David and I were scared, but we put Sofia in God's hands. That was the best place for her to be. At our first appointment at Scottish Rite, we met Dr. Birch. He was a kind and sweet man. After x-rays and examining Sofia, Dr. Birch explained her condition to us in more depth. He then proceeded to tell David and me what the next five years of her life would be like. Sofia would be in a full-body brace for the first year of her life. The hope was that the brace would force the bones of her legs upward and inward in order to create a hip socket. Sofia would be harnessed in the brace 23 hours a day. We would only be able to take her out of the brace one hour a day to massage her legs and bathe her. David and I had to figure out how to change diapers working through the straps of the brace. Dr. Birch continued and stated that when Sofia turned 1 year old, she would have corrective surgery and be placed in a body cast. Can you imagine a 1-year-old in a body cast? How would we change diapers at that point? Once the body cast was removed, Sofia would begin physical therapy. Dr. Birch's concluding statement was hard to hear. He poignantly stated that Sofia would be enduring all of this, "In hopes that she might walk someday." David and I were astonished. We just had the wind knocked out of us. We were sad. We were frightened of the unknown.

There was no time to waste. During her appointment, Sofia was fitted for her first brace. David and I were taught how to put the brace on properly and how to take it off. We were taught the correct way to massage Sofia's little legs. Her legs would be sore due to being in the brace for 23 hours. We were shown the best way to work around the brace in order to change diapers. Just call us Houdini one and two. David and I were told that we would need to bring Sofia back to Scottish Rite every two weeks for x-rays and a check-up to monitor her progress. We were just numb. We went home and processed the information that had been given to us. We prayed. David and I discussed our work schedules, how doctor appointments needed to be arranged, and multiple other issues. But we were ready to dig in and do whatever needed to be done for our little Sofia.

I was sick. Literally. I was in constant pain. I kept telling David that something was not right with me. I called my OB-GYN office more than once and told them I thought something was wrong with me. I always got the same response that I was a first-time parent, and everything I was experiencing was normal. I had been bathing, and without getting graphic, I stunk. I told David, "Something is wrong with me." I called my doctor and insisted on her seeing me. I went to her office, and before she could even examine me, she could smell me. It was disgusting. My doctor immediately knew I had an infection. A really bad infection. I was prescribed antibiotics for the infection inside my body due to the C-section. I would also be taking 800mg of Ibuprofen as well for the constant pain I was experiencing. Sad to say, but I was pretty drugged up and out of it for the first few weeks of Sofia's life. I accompanied David to Sofia's doctor appointments and did what I could do to help with Sofia, which wasn't much. I missed out on the beauty of breastfeeding, which I had longed to do.

With me being sick, this left David to most of the responsibilities of caring for Sofia and for me. David called his sister one day and asked, "Am I supposed to be bathing Sofia?" His sister replied, "I'm on my way over."

I do not believe for one moment that God caused me to get sick. Although I do believe He allowed it. You might ask why. In the beginning, David had been so adamant about us not using donor sperm in order for me to get pregnant. In the end, I think the resulting factor of me becoming so ill was the perfect set-up for David to bond with Sofia. David already loved Sofia, and she was his child. But much later, we both believe that God unveiled a little truth that my sickness turned out to be a huge blessing. David needed that one-on-one time with Sofia. He needed to feel immensely connected to her. He needed her to need him. And she did. A bond was undoubtedly formed between daddy and daughter. I am sad that I missed out on much of those first few weeks of Sofia's life but wouldn't change a thing. The entire situation needed to happen. What at first seemed painful and hard for me as a new mom was, in truth, a blessing for a new dad. Perspective.

One difficult issue was that Sofia could not sleep. The full-body brace that she was required to wear made it impossible for her to get comfortable. I wish you could see a picture of her in the brace. It was needed but truly uncompromising to deal with. The brace left Sofia little room for movement. It forced her legs into a somewhat sitting position in order to press her femur bones towards her body with the hope of causing hip sockets to form. It was not at all enjoyable for our newborn. So how did we remedy the situation? David would turn Sofia face down on his belly. That was the only position that allowed her to get some much-needed rest. Sofia was never in any harm whatsoever of suffocating, but she could sleep peacefully on her daddy's belly.

After several weeks of maneuvering around this brace, trips to Scottish Rite Hospital, and having a baby that was just miserable and uncomfortable all the time, David and I decided we were done. Done! The mere thought of witnessing the struggles Sofia would be experiencing for the next year of her life was heart-rending. Add to that the agonizing thought of the ensuing surgery when she would turn 1 year old and be placed in a body cast. David and I were all in. We were prepared to do whatever we had to do. David and I needed to know we did everything within our power to ensure the possibility that Sofia would be able to walk one day. David and I had a discussion and decided that we would go before our church and fully explain Sofia's prognosis. We would also share the information the doctor had given us regarding the next five years of her life. We would then present Sofia in front of the congregation and have a prayer of healing spoken over her. David and I expressed how we were informed that Sofia might never walk. We then proclaimed that our God is bigger than any diagnosis. We asked everyone at church one Sunday morning to join us in praying for God to heal Sofia that very day. The entire church gathered around us in prayer, and many people laid hands on Sofia. When the prayer was concluded, David and I said with confidence, "She's healed."

The next appointment for Sofia at Scottish Rite Hospital is one that will forever be in our hearts and in our minds. The normal routine was followed. Sofia first had to be checked in. Proceeding that, Sofia was taken to have the normal x-rays done on her hips. She was then placed in an exam room, waiting for the doctor to arrive. As Dr. Birch approached the exam room, you could hear him pick Sofia's patient folder up out of the file holder on the door. A moment or two passed, then he asked the nurse, "What patient am I seeing in here?" The nurse replied, "Sofia Butler." Dr. Birch said, "That's not possible. There's nothing wrong with this child!"

At that moment, Dr. Birch walked in, white as a ghost, with Sofia's current x-rays and the ones taken just two weeks before. He pointed out on the previous x-rays that Sofia's legs were still separated from her body, and no "correction" had begun to happen yet. Afterward, he held up Sofia's newest x-rays and pointed out that she had perfectly formed hip sockets, the femur bones in her legs were connected properly to her hip sockets, and all the tendons and muscles were formed and in correct alignment. There was absolutely nothing wrong with Sofia's legs anymore. She was perfectly formed.

Dr. Birch turned and said, "I can't explain this!" The only truth and reply were that "God healed her." Dr. Birch was told about the prayers for Sofia the previous Sunday during church. He was still in shock. Dr. Birch asked if he could still do check-ups on Sofia until she was 5 years old "just to make sure she was okay." David and I agreed to continue to take Sofia back to Scottish Rite Hospital yearly until she was 5 years old. After Sofia's fifth birthday and hospital visit, she was released from medical care.

What happened with Sofia was the first time in my life that I ever got to witness a miracle. A miracle is something that requires divine intervention in order to manifest. Well, the two sets of x-rays are evidence of God healing Sofia, a miracle. The fertility issues that David and I had come up against resulted in a happy ending. We went through much heartache, but we had a baby. We had Sofia. We were parents. And Sofia was a perfectly healthy baby.

I am saddened that not everyone has the same story as ours. Please know, be that as it may, there are always options when it comes to becoming a parent, and I will tell more of that shortly. David and I were beyond blessed in the way that everything turned out for us. Although, in hindsight, I do not want to negate the fact that there were a couple of years that were pure hell for us. The heart-wrenching, unexpected, unending "bad news" was the biggest issue. Emotional overload. The questions. The financial obligation. There were some hard days, some overwhelming days. David felt our infertility issue was all his fault since he could not have children. He had major issues with self-hate. I sometimes wondered if it was my fault for what I had done in the past, the abortions. Was our lack of being able to conceive my "punishment?" It is amazing how Satan will flood our minds with all types of malicious lies because his intent is to destroy our worth, our hope, and our faith.

Now David and I were and are devout Christians. We should have known better than to allow the enemy to make us question ourselves, right? No. Satan is sly, powerful, manipulative, and he knows our weaknesses. Satan finds little footholds and causes doubt and disunity in marriages and all relationships wherever he can. Do not be dismayed or feel guilty if the enemy has caused you to doubt yourself or to doubt God. That's his job. He is on a rampage because he knows it is just a matter of time until he is permanently discharged from his position.

David and I were overjoyed with Sofia and with being parents. But we also knew we wanted more children to complete our family. With me still being young enough to proceed with an "elderly pregnancy" (sorry, I still laugh at that term), we tried two more procedures. I had talked to David and told him I really did not want to attempt in-vitro fertilization again. I did not want to put my body through that again with no guarantee of a pregnancy. And quite honestly, we did not have the money. In-vitro fertilization is expensive. David and I made the decision and tried two rounds of Intrauterine Insemination, and neither resulted in a pregnancy. We were happy with our Sofia and decided to explore adoption. We had no idea what we were in for.

Whatever hard season you may be going through, keep going. Do not allow the lies of the enemy to get you stuck in life. When we found out that David was sterile, we could have given up on having children. David and I could have decided that it was just our lot in life to be a childless couple. When we found out that Sofia was born handicapped and might not ever walk, David and I could have made the decision to back out of the battle and do what we could to make Sofia's life as comfortable as possible, have a ramp for a wheelchair installed at our house, and given up.

Now, if Sofia would not have been healed, I can assure you David and I would not have retreated. We would have made sure that she never saw herself as a victim and inspired her to do whatever she put her mind to. If you do not know the story of Nick Vujicic, you should definitely look him up on the internet. He has been a guest on the television show I work for multiple times, and he will inspire you. Nick was born without arms or legs, but his parents insisted on him having a normal childhood. Nick swam and played sports. Without arms or legs? Yes. Nick is married and has children and travels the world telling others about the amazing love of God. My battle cry to you is, "Don't give up." Life is full of hills and valleys. Don't allow life to keep you down. When you find yourself at a crossroads in life, look at all your options. There are answers to your issues. You just need to look for them. Do not listen to the voice of the enemy. Listen to the voice of hope. God can get you through any circumstance that you come up against.

"Symphony"

-By: Switch featuring Dillon Chase

"Up Again"

-By: Dan Bremnes

Chapter 8

STD = Sexually Transmitted Disease
Better Yet: STD = Shame Totally Disarmed

With all due honesty, I originally wanted to save this chapter for later. If your curiosity is elevated, good. As I proclaimed in the "Introduction" of this book, it's all about perspective. This is truly an example of where pain and passion collided in my life, but the reality of that intersection will not be unveiled until a later chapter. Stay tuned.

When David and I decided to adopt, the first thought that made the most sense to us was the fact that there were so many children in the CPS system that needed loving parents. Our gut told us to start there. We were not concerned with the race of our future child or children. We were open to black, white, Hispanic, Asian, and so forth. We just wanted a child or children to complete our family. Our desire was to share our love and give a home to a child or children in need. Sofia was exceedingly excited at the prospect of a sibling or two. David and I wanted to grow our family. I most likely could write a book on each chapter of this book, but I am trying to keep the information concise.

David and I enrolled and went through the entire training course required when anyone intended to foster to adopt. There were numerous classes that took place in the evenings after a long day at work. There was an enormous amount of knowledge and preparation that was presented to us. David and I finished the in-depth training and received our certification. Yay!

One more milestone under our belts as we forged toward becoming parents, again. Regrettably, in a very short amount of time, it was obvious that going through CPS would not be the right route for us. We were unimaginably sad, but we prayed and decided to withdraw from the program. The biggest issue was that we could not risk falling in love with a child that could be taken away from us at any moment. That would have been catastrophic to us.

David was continuously busy working full-time at the television show we were employed at and basically volunteering full-time at our church as well. I began researching many different adoption agencies from all over the United States. Every single agency had different qualifications for prospective adoptive parents. The search got really crazy and time-consuming. Reading through all these websites and trying to figure out what country to adopt from required careful investigation. Other concerns were: did David and I both meet the qualifications listed at any particular adoption agency, and could we afford the financial obligations? According to some agencies, I was already too old to adopt because I was 40 or beyond. I understand the agencies want to make sure the parents live long enough to raise the child, but I was not 99 years old. It would be okay to laugh here. With other agencies, David weighed too much. Again, I respect the fact that an agency has the child's interest at heart and desires healthy adoptive parents. I am not complaining. It was all just a bit mind-boggling. The qualifications, finances, travel times, and everything involved were just so much to sort through. I was exploring domestic adoption agencies as well as international adoption agencies. At the conclusion of months of research, David and I narrowed our interest to Haiti and China.

After analyzing the option of China, I was regretful to find out the wait time for the adoption process in China at the time was four to six years. Sofia was already 4 years old, and David and I wanted our children to be closer in age. I inadvertently came across an agency that had Taiwan listed. I was unfamiliar with Taiwan, so I commenced on some reading.

Taiwan is an island just off the coast of China. Taiwan is officially part of the Republic of China. I then discovered the wait time to adopt a child from Taiwan was only 9 to 12 months. Yes, months, not years. I was thrilled with this new information. David and I prayed about it and started the adoption process to adopt a daughter from Taiwan. By process, I mean the beginning of countless amounts of paperwork and trying to figure out how we were going to pay for an adoption.

I always worried about money. Always. Sorry to say that, but it is true. I was responsible for stewarding all the finances for David and me. With that being said, I knew how much we did not have for an adoption. There was a day I was completely stressing about everything, mostly the money issue, and clear as day I heard God say, "You wouldn't think twice about spending $40,000.00 on a car." My reply to God was, "You created me and know how frugal I am, so You, of all people, know that I would indeed think twice about spending $40,000.00 on a car, but I get your point!" After that, I just knew God would take care of our family, the finances, and the entire adoption process.

There is frankly a tremendous amount of details of the adoption process that I will not go into. But here is the part that has to do with the title of this chapter. Without a doubt, the government of Taiwan wanted to make sure that anyone adopting one of their citizens would be people that were in good health. David and I were both required to have complete medical physicals. I was first to make an appointment to see my doctor. I completed my physical exam and had blood drawn for testing as well. My results came back. I was in tip-top good health. Yay! David made his appointment and had a physical and blood work done as well.

One day David and I were in the parking lot at our fitness gym, and David's phone rang. It was David's doctor's office. We were asked to come into the office for the results. When my results were in, I had just gotten a phone call saying I was all good. David asked what this was about. He was told that it would probably be better if he came in for the results and if I came with him. Really? We wanted to drive straight to the doctor's office. You don't tell someone something like that, then make him wait. Luckily we were able to go in the next day, if I remember correctly. David and I were both literally sick to our stomachs. Did David have cancer? Did he not pass the physical, so our chances at adopting from Taiwan just went down the drain? Was it something worse? What on earth were we walking into?

Dr. Witherspoon welcomed us with his warm, sweet spirit as always. He asked David and me to sit down. I seriously thought I was about to throw up or pass out. Either possibility was better than waiting for whatever was about to be dropped on us. We were accustomed to receiving not-so-good news in the offices of our doctors. The good doctor pulled out some paperwork. This was all the information on David's blood work. Dr. Witherspoon apologized and said that he had made a mistake in the request for the lab regarding David's blood work. He had checked off everything that needed to be tested, but then he accidentally checked the box to have David's blood tested for STDs. David and I were sitting there thinking, "And your point?" It was at that moment that Dr. Witherspoon told us that David had tested positive for Herpes.

David turned white as a ghost and looked very confused. I don't know what look I had on my face, but Dr. Witherspoon said, "Now wait a minute…" David interrupted and looked at me and just said, "I have not cheated on you!" I then turned to the doctor and asked, "How is this possible? David and I had both been tested for STDs before getting married. Each of us had been previously sexually active, and the tests came back negative."

The doctor responded that, sometimes, the virus would not show up immediately after being contracted. He added that in some cases, it might take some time for the virus to show up in the blood. Dr. Witherspoon then tried to start talking to David and me about the situation, but I think we were both in shock. The good doctor tried to tell us that it was not as bad as we thought. He began informing us about the Herpes Virus. "It can't kill you. It can't make you sick. It can't actually harm you in any way." Dr. Witherspoon said one in six people have contracted an STD, and about 50% of those people don't even know they have one, as with David. Dr. Witherspoon then looked at me and said, "You need to get tested. I'll write up the lab request right now, and you can go down the hall to get the test."

What? My thoughts were, "What the heck is happening here? How is this possible? We are not having symptoms. We were tested before we got married. Neither of us had cheated on the other. If this wasn't bad enough, was this going to keep us from adopting a child?" We were assured that this information would not be shared because it was not one of the requested blood tests. Talk about getting the breath knocked out of us one more time.

Without dragging things out, I tested positive as well. Herpes. Herpes Virus. Herpes Simplex. HSV-2. Wow! Well, we were glad that David wasn't dying or anything, but Herpes was not at all on our radars, and we were in shock. David later told me he was actually relieved that my test came back positive. He honestly felt like we might have split up if I was negative. And I get that. There is such a negative stigma attached to STDs. I know this to be true because David and I were kids of the '80s when HIV-AIDS was somewhat new and terrifying. Back then, HIV seemed like a death sentence, and it was for so many people. But Herpes? We had heard of it but really did not know anything about it. We were still totally freaked out. We both felt like we now had this horrible "label" on us. Dr. Witherspoon was so kind and encouraging, and he gave us much-needed information on HSV-2. But it really didn't ease any of what we were feeling at the time.

Now some of the information you might read on the internet about Herpes is not true; some of it is misleading, some of it is terrifying, some of it is hard to believe, some of it is confusing, and a lot of it is true. If you are reading this, I believe it is imperative that you are informed on the facts regarding Herpes. Why? Because you probably know someone that has Herpes, although you may not know it. That person might not even know it if they are non-symptomatic. I chose not to only get information to share with you off the internet for the abovementioned reasons. I instead decided to interview a professional that is familiar with the facts. So, what did Margie Chung, RNC, FNP of Sandknop Health Group, have to disclose about Herpes? Before I move forward with that, let me just add that God is still in the healing business, and this is not the end of my and David's story regarding this issue of Herpes. Let us proceed with the questions I asked Margie Chung:

1. **What are the two types of Herpes?**

   Herpes Type I, Herpes Type II, and Herpes Foster. (Yes, she had to correct me. I thought there were only two types. Herpes Foster has to do with Chicken Pox and Shingles, so we will not be discussing that one.)

2. **Can you briefly describe each?**

   Herpes Type I: Herpes virus is typically responsible for causing cold sores and canker sores in the nose and mouth.

   Herpes Type II: Herpes Virus is typically responsible for causing genital herpes.

3. **How do you contract each type of Herpes?**

   Herpes Type I: Oral-to-oral contact; there are, however, cases of genital herpes that are Type I from oral–genital contact.

   Herpes Type II: Sexually transmitted; through skin-to-skin contact.

4. **How common is Herpes Type II?**

   Occurs in about 12% to 20% of the population. (That number may sound small, but it is not. According to the CDC, 12% is one in eight people in the U.S. has Herpes Type II, and as many as 90% are unaware that they have the virus.)

5. **What are the symptoms of Herpes Type II?**

   Pain and itching caused by blister-like lesions in the genital area. You may also have no signs (or symptoms) and be contagious.

6. **Is Herpes Type II curable?**

   No. There are medicines that can prevent or shorten breakouts. These meds can be taken daily to reduce (not eliminate) the chances of transmission to partner.

7. **What are the treatments for Herpes Type II:**

   Medicines—antivirals such as Acyclovir, Famciclovir, or Valacyclovir. Anti-inflammatories such as Ibuprofen, Advil, and Aleve.

8. **Is Herpes Type II deadly?**

   No.

9. **Is Herpes Type II harmful to your body?**

   No. If, however, a pregnant woman has an active breakout, a C-section will be performed to reduce the risk of transmission to the baby as they pass through the birth canal.

10. **Can a person with Herpes Type II lead a normal life?**

    Yes.

11. **Final thoughts?**

    The diagnosis of a positive Herpes (genital) infection is a hard one to share with patients, especially if they have not had a breakout. STDs continue to have social taboo, so there are emotional issues surrounding this diagnosis.

Thank you, Margie Chung, RNC, FNP, for answering my questions and explaining Herpes in a simple form. If you would like more information, there are obviously multiple websites discussing Herpes. One I have referred to in the past is ashasexualhealth.org.

This was the most challenging chapter to include in this book. I decided to completely expose my personal life here for multiple reasons. I wanted people to know that an STD diagnosis is not the end of the world. I desired that people know the truth and facts regarding Herpes. You cannot contract the herpes virus by eating or drinking after a person that has the virus. The virus is not something "in the air" that you could contract just from being around someone that has herpes. The only way to contract genital herpes is through sexual contact.

Herpes is completely treatable. Do not live in fear. I included the symptoms for the basic reason that so many individuals are unaware they even have herpes. But most of all, I wanted to be a voice for anyone that has been diagnosed with herpes and is allowing shame or fear to steal their life. Do not become anti-social. Do not give up on meeting someone and falling in love. You need to be honest regarding your diagnosis, but you can also present the facts about the virus. It's hard. Trust me, I know. But as you will find out in a later chapter, herpes does not exclude you from life or love. God can take things we see as setbacks or unexpected issues that just slap us upside the head and use it for His glory. If one person that has been diagnosed with herpes finds an ounce of hope after reading this chapter, then it was totally worth exposing another one of my secrets. God is good.

"Yes He Can"

-By: Cain

Chapter 9

The Ups And Downs Of Adoption And Marriage
The Reality And Need Of Intervention
And Boundaries

After months of paperwork, a home study, payments, more paperwork, medical exams, payments, and paperwork, fingerprinting, background checks, and even more paperwork and payments, David and I were done with the adoption process for the most part. Payments would continue for some time longer, but at that point, we were just waiting to be matched with a child. Yes! David and I had requested a female child from the age of 12 months to 2 years old. We wanted Sofia and our new daughter to be somewhat close enough in age to truly enjoy growing up together. The waiting game commenced…tick-tock.

David and I were at home when the call came through. Our adoption representative, Dina, had called to give us the good news. She told us that there was a child that was available to us. Dina reminded us that she was aware that we had requested a 12-month to a 2-year-old girl, but a baby had just been brought into the orphanage. David and I were next on the list of adoptive parents. The baby was only a few weeks old. Dina then asked if she could send us a picture of the baby girl, and of course, David and I said yes. As we had Dina on the phone and a baby picture coming up on our computer screen, our eyes just locked on this baby. She was small. She was beautiful. She was precious. She was ours. Dina asked, "Do you want her?" Are you kidding? Don't send us a picture of a baby and think you need to ask us if we want her. Of course, we wanted her. Without hesitation, we told Dina, "Yes, we want her!"

Dina paused and informed us that she was required to disclose specific issues of this baby. These disclosures had to be presented to us prior to us formally agreeing to accept this child. What now? Since David and I had requested a healthy child, Dina was obligated to share the child's health issues. David and I had no idea what was about to be revealed to us. Our faith was strong, and our hearts were steady. We fell in love with this baby as soon as we saw her picture.

Dina let us know that the baby's birth mother was in prison. The biological mom was incarcerated due to drug use. Once the baby was born, and regular tests were administered on her, it was discovered that the baby had Hepatitis C. Hep C is a disease caused by a virus that infects the liver and can be deadly. Not only that, the disease can be spread several ways, one being if you come in contact with blood from an infected person. Since David and I were already parents, we were very familiar with the cuts and scrapes little ones get, so there was a potential, a possibility, this child could possibly transmit this disease to David, me, or Sofia at some point. We were told that the baby's birth mom possibly contracted the disease through sharing needles due to her drug habit.

David and I just looked at each other, and we knew. People have all kinds of "incurable" viruses. People had all kinds of diseases. People had all kinds of undesirable issues. But these issues do not make them any less of a person or any less deserving of love. This little baby girl was dealt a bad hand in life, but she was perfect in our eyes. She was meant to be our daughter. We told Dina that the Dallas-Fort Worth Metroplex had some amazing children's hospitals. David and I did not care what medical issues this baby had, we wanted her, and we would provide any and all the help that she needed. No virus was going to keep us from loving this child and bringing her into our family. Dina seemed surprised. She told us to think about it because it would be a big responsibility because Hepatitis C is a transmittable virus. We told Dina that we did not need to think about it. She insisted that we take 24 hours then get back to her. The phone conversation ended, and David and I did what we always did…we prayed.

David and I thanked God for bringing this little baby, this child, our child, into our lives. We asked God to watch over her and protect her. We prayed for the orphanage workers that were caring for her until we could travel to Taiwan to get her. We prayed that the adoption process be quick and easy. Then we prayed a specific prayer of healing. Not that God needed to be reminded, but we reminded God of how He healed Sofia. It was a miracle. We then asked God to extend this healing power to our new baby. Just as God had adopted us into His Kingdom, His family, and loved us, we were adopting this little sick girl into our family. David and I asked that she receive the same miraculous healing power over her body that Sofia did. It was a simple but powerful prayer full of thanks and expectation.

David and I felt that the issue was settled. With that being said, we were not surprised at all when Dina called us back in a couple of weeks and told us that the doctors were doing some routine tests on the baby and her blood work came back clear. There was absolutely no trace of Hep C in her body. Some people would say that her body just "cleared" the virus. The main religions in Taiwan are Buddhism and Taoism. Dina told us that the people caring for the baby said that the gods healed the baby because of our willingness to take a contagious, sick child. Ying and Yang. We knew that the one true God showered His favor and blessing on her, and He healed her. I do not mean any disrespect to the religions of Buddhism or Taoism. But David and I prayed to our God and believed her healing came from Him.

David and I have multiple friends who have adopted from countries all over the world. And sadly, some of their stories were not good ones. We were blessed in that everything went smoothly with our adoption. The agency we utilized was top-notch. David and I had picked a name for our baby, Lily-Grace. The orphanage was amazing and e-mailed us pictures every month, allowing us to see Lily's growth and progress. The initial thought was that we would be able to get Lily around the time she would be nine months old. I honestly do not know if David and I were the most excited or Sofia was. Sofia could not wait to get her little sister home. She was already talking about all of the fun things she would do with Lily and how she would help take care of her. Although Sofia let us know that she was not the least bit interested in changing diapers. Can you blame her?

Then it happened. The call came. But it wasn't the call we were expecting. Dina told us that some of the adoption laws had recently changed in Taiwan. Dina explained that the orphanage would have to offer Lily to three domestic couples first. If none of the couples in Taiwan wanted Lily, then she would be ours. Ours? What? She was already ours. We had already named her and everything. Dina said her hands were tied, and this process was happening. Wow! What a punch in the gut. Lily was ours. Period. Dina seemed very calm and told us we had nothing to worry about. What? Confused. When David and I asked why she would imply such a thing, Dina gave us a surprising answer. She told us that Lily had three strikes against her. What? Dina went on to state that Lily's birth mom was in prison, and criminal behavior and prison were considered very shameful in the Asian culture. This information would have to be presented to the three sets of prospective parents. Dina added the fact that the birth mom was a drug user, and that was also shameful in the Asian culture. Lastly, Dina pointed out that due to the fact that Lily was native to the island of Taiwan, and she had dark skin, she would not be wanted because families preferred the lighter Chinese skin. What? You are kidding! Yay for us but how sad that this child was being judged for things she had no control over. This made me think of my own childhood. I wanted to make sure that Lily was loved for exactly who she is, who God created her to be.

The process did not take long. David and I received the message that Lily was ours. She was offered to three families in Taiwan, and they all passed on her. This was good news to us. She was already ours anyway. I promise you I am not being egotistical in any way. David and I just knew that God intended that Lily would be our child. Amen! From that moment on, it was just a waiting process. Waiting on the phone call to go to Taiwan to get our baby girl. Tick Tock Tick Tock Tick Tock, ring! When David and I received the phone call that it was time to purchase our plane tickets to Taiwan, I just about jumped out of my skin. I was ready to hold our baby girl. Happy mama dance.

Due to the changes in law, it turned out that we arrived in Taiwan to get Lily four days after her first birthday. Once David and I got checked into our hotel and rested for one day, we were met by our interpreter, Jenny, the following morning. Jenny would be traveling with us to the orphanage and escorting us around Taiwan for the following two weeks. We were in Taiwan. We were about to get our baby girl. We were exhausted. We were excited. All was well in the world.

I could go into every single detail of that day, "Gotcha Day." The compressed version is that David and I were met in our hotel lobby by Jenny in order to board the train for Kaohsiung, Taiwan, where the orphanage was located. The two-hour train ride seemed to go by quickly. Jenny was sweet and talkative. She shared some history of Taiwan as we were traveling and described the landscape as we passed by. Once in Kaohsiung, Jenny hailed a taxi for us and had us driven to a local restaurant for lunch. In the city of Taipei, where our hotel was located, there were many people who spoke English. In Kaohsiung, Jenny had to speak for us, which included ordering our food. After lunch, Jenny escorted David and me to the orphanage to meet Lily and complete our family. Upon arrival at the orphanage, David and I were introduced to the staff and given a tour. We were then taken to a room and asked to sit down on the floor. Lily was brought in. She was sat on the ground as Jenny interpreted between David and me with the woman that ran the orphanage. Lily was definitely checking David and me out. We spent about two hours at the orphanage. Lily became comfortable with David and me, and we both had our chance to hold her. As we prepared to leave the orphanage, several of the young staff members were crying. Jenny asked us if the staff could hold Lily one last time and say goodbye. I handed Lily over.

It was a sweet moment. It was obvious that Lily had been loved during her first year of life in the orphanage. As we drove away in the taxi, our family felt complete. David and I had Lily. She was ours. My heart was filled with love and warmth as I held my daughter and kissed her goodnight that evening. Every moment of that day was precious. We laughed, we cried, we got to meet the people that cared for Lily the first year of her life. They laughed, they cried. It was a long, emotional, beautiful day. We had our Lily.

With the incredible technology of the day, David and I were able to have video chats daily with Sofia and with David's mom, Joyce, who was watching Sofia for us. Sofia could not travel to Taiwan with us because she was in school. David shot a video every day, edited it, and then loaded it up on our YouTube channel every night. This allowed our family and friends to share in our day-to-day experiences with Lily and feel like they were participants of our time in Taiwan. Those videos are priceless to us now, and Lily loves to watch them.

David and I had a wonderful two weeks in Taiwan, but we were ready to get back to Texas and see our other baby girl, Sofia. We had never been away from her for such a long time. It had been a long, strenuous trip. We also had a 1-year-old that wanted to walk all over the plane. Luckily, Lily did sleep a lot during our travel back to America. We knew there would be family and friends to meet us at the airport upon arrival. When we walked through the security doors and into the baggage claim area, Sofia was the first person to run over and grab her little sister and give her a big hug. Lily had no idea who all these people were, and she had a tight grip on me. By the way, I had her saying "Mama" before we ever left Taiwan. Pretty good for a child that had never even heard English before.

We were back in America. We were in Texas. We were home. We had our two girls, and our family was complete. Life was good. Or was it?

Don't get me wrong. We were overjoyed, ecstatic, happy, and blessed. However, it did not take long to realize that something with Lily wasn't quite "right." I do not know how to explain it any other way than that. David and

I knew that all children were different. We knew Sofia and Lily would have different personalities, different likes and dislikes, different a lot of stuff. That's just life. We are all made differently, uniquely. But that wasn't it. Not long after we returned home, we noticed Lily could be very violent. At first, David and I just assumed that due to the fact Lily had been in an orphanage for the first year of her life, she might have had to fight for attention. Maybe she didn't like sharing us with Sofia since she had had David and me to herself for two weeks in Taiwan. But things got worse. Most of the inflictions were directed at Sofia. Lily would pinch Sofia, bite her, hit her, throw things at her, and just pull wads of Sofia's hair out if she could get hold of Sofia's hair. Sofia was being physically hurt. David and I tried to stop Lily, and we had asked Sofia not to hurt Lily in return. But we could tell that these actions were having a negative impact on Sofia. Sofia loved Lily but had to avoid her at times which just made Lily more intent to get Sofia's attention in any way that she could. That "way" was usually by hurting Sofia.

David and I had never experienced anger issues with Sofia, so we were completely lost and had no idea what to do regarding Lily. We had a number of well-meaning parents tell us that the episodes were an early onset of the "terrible twos." Uh, no, we were not accepting that. David and I did our best to control Lily, to re-direct her attention, to soothe her, but she continued to get worse. David and I were admittedly excited when the time came for Lily's two-year check-up because we wanted to address the issues with her pediatrician. During the examination, David and I were told by the doctor that Lily was perfectly healthy. The "diagnosis" that we were given regarding her outbursts was that Lily just had a lot of energy and would grow out of it. You don't say!

Well, she wasn't growing out of it; in fact, she began getting violent with David as well. I cannot even begin to express to you what our home life had transformed into. Our daily routine was a constant balancing act of a happy home life and a war zone. I assure you I am not exaggerating. One never knew what would "set Lily off," so home life was difficult and emotionally heavy. The situation was beyond sad and exhausting. David and I had no idea how to help our Lily, nor did we know how to explain to Sofia what was going on because we did not have a clue. Lily had a laugh that brightened the darkest day. She had a smile that was drenched in warmth. She was full of energy and always wanted to help with whatever task anyone might be doing. Yes, Lily was sweet, kind, cuddly and loving…until she wasn't. It seemed as if she had a dual personality, and we had no idea what to do.

As I mentioned earlier, David and I had unfortunately experienced marital issues from day one. I realize that all couples, married or not, come up against challenges, but David and I never seemed to get much of a break. There was always some issue causing tension and exhaustion in our marriage. The atmosphere in our home was pushing David, Sofia, and me to our limits. We tried everything to help Lily, but it was not uncommon for her to throw two-hour screaming fits every single night. None of us knew the cause of these eruptions. And what broke David and my heart even more was that our sweet 5-year-old Sofia was withdrawing because she was, in a sense, losing her parents. It required both David and me to keep the household running. One kept an eye on Lily while the other cooked, cleaned, and helped Sofia with homework. Before David and I adopted Lily, we would take Sofia to kiddie concerts, plays, the Dallas Arboretum, festivals, and such fun things. We could not do such activities any longer because we had no idea when Lily might have a meltdown. I cannot remember who in the household came up with the name, but her outbursts came to be referred to as hulk smashes. The Incredible Hulk was known for his temper and path of destruction. Please do not think my family was being cruel by calling Lily's outbursts such a name. If you knew what we had been experiencing in our home, you would understand. It was our way of letting each other know that Lily was currently out of control.

As if the issues we had already been dealing with were not enough, there was the reality that David and I were constantly exhausted. I worked full-time with long hours as a television producer. David worked in television and as a minister. He basically had two full-time jobs. He was eventually appointed the Associate Pastor at our church. Being a Pastor, it was not uncommon for David to receive calls any time, day or night, from members of our church. David, Sofia, Lily, and I lived in Rockwall, Texas, at the time. But David and I worked in Euless, Texas, so we were commuting an average of three hours a day. Yes, I said three hours per day, Monday through Friday, driving in rush hour traffic. I normally worked 12 to 13 hours on Tuesdays when we taped television shows. That meant David and I had to drive to work separately on Tuesdays. Our lives were spinning out of control. No one was aware of it, though, because we always put on smiles and put our best foot forward. David was a pastor, and I was a pastor's wife, so we had to act like we had it all together. Hmmm, sound familiar? I was pretending to be okay when I obviously was not. Not in the least bit okay. And neither was David. And neither was Sofia. And neither was Lily. Our family was falling apart for various reasons, and we could not stop it. Or could we?

I know this chapter is about Lily's adoption, but I need to interject a few things before I move on. David and I were having problems. Major problems. Serious problems. But no one knew it. There was one specific issue that continually caused friction between David and me. That friction led to escalating distance between us. That distance led to arguments between us. Those arguments led to brokenness. That brokenness led to a feeling of hopelessness. David could not see my point of view on this issue and adamantly disagreed with me. It was an issue that continually hurt me. It hurt Sofia and Lily. I had suggested we go to counseling multiple times, but David rejected the idea. We had tried counseling once before with our Senior Pastor and his wife, but David said he felt like we were all ganging up against him. Another time during counseling, I was just emotionally out of it. Needless to say, returning to counseling at our church was not a good idea, and we knew it. David was not interested in counseling, so I just dropped it. We continued on and pressed forward in life. But the pressing forward only caused more pressure between us. In a later chapter, I will explain the one issue that caused such ongoing tension between David and me.

Please do not get me wrong. David and I did have many good times within our marriage, but we also experienced an enormous number of bad times. Really hard, difficult times. I realize all couples have challenges in marriage. I am not naïve about that. David and I just had one thing after another hit us. And we may not have always handled situations in the best manner possible, but we were doing the best that we could. Or at least we thought we were. I knew David loved me. I loved him. Even so, add all the other issues to the pile…commuting, Joyce not always agreeing with us on certain issues, trying to balance church and home life, workload, Lily's issue, whatever that was…and we were all falling apart. It was like our entire family was deteriorating. David started getting angry. I started getting bitter. He threw himself into what he knew: work and ministry. I began to withdraw more and more.

David's dad, Tom, passed away just a few months before we went to Taiwan to get Lily. Tom's death was a devastating loss to all of us. And this was just the beginning of tremendous loss in the family. The impact of continuous heartache, confusion, distance, and loss was taking its toll on our family, our marriage, and each of us as individuals. The sad truth is that when you do not address these significant events and get help sorting through the pain, it can begin to destroy you, and you don't even truly realize it's happening on some level. You think you can handle it. You think your faith will pull you through. In reality, you're drowning, and the process can be fatal.

David and I were mentally, physically, and spiritually exhausted. I need to back up one moment. Circumstances between David and I had reached an all-time low. It was not that we were not trying. We were just consumed, drained, and burnt out. I had prayed and prayed and begged God to intervene and change, fix, redeem, transform, and renew the relationship between David and me. I suggested counseling again to David. I truly felt David and I needed counseling individually and as a couple. We had both experienced so much trauma in our lives. I was at the point where I just felt like David and I could no longer continue in life, in marriage, as we had been… merely surviving for the previous years. It was not healthy for any of us in our family, and nothing was changing. David still did not feel comfortable with the idea of counseling. Without outside help, some type of counseling, was divorce the next step? I was confused, sad, and scared.

I was not expecting the phone call that my Uncle James had passed away. David and I decided I would make the two-hour trip back home and he would stay with Sofia and Lily. I had met my mom and dad at their house to make the drive to attend the viewing on Friday night. When we arrived back at my parent's home, I was ready for bed when David called me with the news that his brother Thomas had passed away. Thomas was only 45 years old. He had been sitting at the table eating with his wife and two daughters when he had a massive heart attack. I immediately grabbed my things and headed home. We made it through the funeral. It was taxing on everyone. So unexpected and sudden. David had lost his father and his brother approximately 19 months apart. Death. The loss of life. The loss of loved ones. It's hard. It's permanent. You can't go back. I think what we were experiencing changed us all. And because of what I had gone through in my past, honesty was and is huge to me. It was time to be honest with David.

After some time had passed, David and I were out to dinner one evening. I felt that I needed to tell him that I had seriously been considering leaving him just prior to the weekend Thomas had passed away. He looked shocked, but he listened. For the first time in a long time, he listened. I listed the reasons and why I had come to the decision I had. He owned up to his actions and apologized and promised things would get better. I said I would try harder as well. I thought this was a new beginning for us. And it was, for a while.

If you have adopted a child and it may not be the entirely beautiful scenario you thought it would be, pause. I have heard horror stories of adoptions. I have heard of parents returning kids they had adopted. There is no judgment here from me. I have also listened to beautiful adoption stories. Adoption is just another thing in life that can have its ups and downs. I don't know if I should share this or not. It may cause you to think I am a horrible person. But I promised to be honest in this book, so I feel the need to share this. On one night that Lily was having a complete breakdown, and I just could not handle it anymore, I walked into another room and started crying. I asked God why. After all that David and I had already gone through and we just wanted to adopt a healthy child, why? Lily was obviously not mentally healthy. Her violent outbursts were unnerving all of us. How much more hard knocks could we take in life? Why, God, would you send us a child that had such serious issues? As I was emotionally exhausted, crying, and talking to God, I clearly heard His answer. He replied, "Because I knew I could trust you with her." And by "you," I knew God meant David and me. And I knew what God meant.

You hear so many stories of child abuse and neglect. You even hear of parents causing the deaths of their children in some cases. God knew he could trust us with Lily, and we would never stop loving her and would do everything we could to help her. I do not say any of this to give David and me a pat on our backs. I say this because God always has a plan. Our family was struggling, but we still loved Lily. She was our child, and we would not turn our backs on her. But David and I needed help with her. We needed help in our marriage. There was a need to set boundaries in our marriage and prioritize our family over our schedules. There are often times in our lives that we will be forced to make choices and set boundaries. Change is often needed in order to breathe again.

"Breathe"

-By: Jonny Diaz

Chapter 10

ADHD: Finally A Diagnosis
At Last: Steps In The Right Direction

Things began to escalate with Lily and her violent tendencies. She did not act out on Sofia as much but turned her rage more towards David. Although we all felt Lily's anger in one demonstration or another, Lily's outbursts or "Hulk Smashes" were just the mountaintop to all the other issues that David and I were dealing with. Regretfully, things became heavy at home again. David and I were so tired and weary that one day when we were on the way to Joyce's house, we were stopped at a red light, and David and I both fell asleep in the car. Seriously, we were at a stoplight, and in the amount of time that the light was red, we both fell asleep. We were awakened by the car behind us honking at us. That's dangerous. That is beyond dog-tired exhausted. I guess the only reason the car stayed stopped was that David's foot was tight on the brake. Early mornings, getting kids ready, commuting three hours a day, full workloads along with not getting enough sleep and dysfunction at home were now even affecting our health and safety.

I had brought up the possibility of us moving closer to work multiple times, but David was not interested in moving. Once more, he had been at the church we were attending since he was 9 years old. David had been the youth pastor for years prior to being moved up to the position of Associate Pastor. For most of the years in which he had worked for the church, he was not paid; he volunteered. David was eventually offered a small monthly payment for everything he did for the church. He loved his church and church family, but the main thing that kept us living near the church was the promise of being brought on full-time.

Serving as a full-time pastor was David's dream. The promise of future employment is what made us willing to commute for hours every single day. This situation was an ongoing issue between David and me. We were depleted all the time. I felt like we were absentee parents and missing so much of Sofia's and Lily's childhoods due to our hours on the road. David was killing himself working two jobs. This went on for years. David was told that the church could not afford to offer him a full-time salary but was working towards that goal. We heard this year after year, and David did not feel released to leave the church just yet.

As David and I were sitting in church one morning, an announcement was made about an investment that the church would be acquiring. This investment was quite expensive. It was not something that the church necessarily needed or would add value to the church. Once David and I left church that day, we had a long discussion. We were a bit bewildered, and this investment did not sit well with either of us. We had been told for years that the church did not have the finances to bring David on full-time, but then this large investment was made. I think after that incident, David began to question some priorities of the church and the promises that had been made to him for so many years that were not happening.

We still had all the issues with Lily and a million other things going on. I continued to pray and fast and pray some more. The situation at home was not good. Everyone was tired. We still did not know what was going on with Lily. There was no time for David and me to go on dates which, as we all know, is an important factor in a marriage. The commute was killing me. The commute was affecting us all in a negative way. And one day, I had just had it. I missed my little girls so much. I felt like I wasn't a good mom because I was always so tired. I told David, "If you want to stay here and chase a dream that I have supported you on for years now, you can, but we are missing our babies grow up. And I am moving closer to work. You can stay here, or you can come with me." This may seem like a horribly mean statement to make to a spouse, but it wasn't meant to be. The reality about our lives, or lack thereof, had just come to a head, and change was necessary if we were all going to survive this thing called life. We weren't living. We were just going through the motions. We were merely existing. Our marriage and family life were going down the tubes…fast.

Our weekly routine was chaotic and beyond busy. Sofia was enrolled in Heritage Christian Academy in Rockwall, Texas. When David had started receiving a small payment from the church, we decided to use that money to put Sofia in school early. HCA had a full-day school program starting at three years of age. David and I would wake up between 5:00 and 5:30 am. I would get myself ready then wake Sofia up. While Sofia was getting ready and eating breakfast, David would drive to his parent's house about 15 minutes away to drop Lily off, come back home, and then we would take Sofia to school at 7:00 am for before school care. Our commute to work would be anywhere between one hour and one and a half hours, depending on traffic. We had to drive through Dallas during rush hour, which meant stop-and-go traffic. And if there was a wreck along the way, we were prepared to be parked on the highway for some amount of time. David and I each put in an eight-hour day unless it was a Tuesday when I worked 12 to 13 hours.

As I mentioned before, on Tuesdays, David and I had to drive to work separately. The weekly work schedule required taping a week's worth of shows on Tuesday evenings in front of an audience, and I had to be there. Tuesdays were long workdays for me. On the other days, David and I would leave work between 4:30 and 5:00 pm, commute back to his mom's house, pick up Sofia and Lily, drive to our house, cook dinner, eat, do homework if needed, get the kids bathed and try to get to bed at a decent hour, and then do it all over again the next day.

We were missing so much of the kids' lives due to being on the road commuting so much that I couldn't take it anymore. I had dreamed of being a mom for most of my life, and it took so much to get these precious children. Sofia and Lily deserved to have their parents for more than a couple rushed hours a day. When I told David I was moving, it finally clicked with him, and he said, "You're right." So, David decided to move with me. Yay! Once again, an opening for a fresh new start. Amen!

God always has a plan. And His timing is always right, even if we can't see it at the time. David and I agreed to move. There was a new community being built that we drove by every day on our way to work. This place was only three miles from our job. During this time of transition was when Joyce was diagnosed with cancer. She would not be able to watch Sofia and Lily anymore, which in some way made the move easier for David. Our decision to put our house on the market and move from Rockwall to Arlington, Texas was a "finally" to some people who could not believe we had made that commute for 12 years. But there were others that were not so kind and supportive. David and I were just ready to move on and get some much-needed family time back in our lives.

Rockwall was a hot market, and our house sold in two days. This was wonderful news. David and I were not even bothered by the fact that we had not even begun our search for a new home, and we had thirty days to find one. We had stopped by the community near our work and looked at some houses. The houses were a bit steep for our budget. Since I was the one who handled our finances, I told David I really did not know if we could move into this community. But that did not keep us from dreaming or looking at houses.

There was one house we repeatedly looked at. The builder's representative became very familiar with us and just handed us the keys to the house when we stopped by the model home. I told David we could most likely make things work if we bought this house, but we wouldn't have much money left to live on and enjoy life. I broke the budget down for David so he understood the situation we would be in if we purchased this house. Then it happened. One Thursday night, we received a call. The builder representative told us she knew we loved the house we had been looking at. She then informed us that the builder needed to unload this house. It was the last house in Phase A, and no one was putting in any offers for it. The builder needed to get it off the books so the company could start building houses in Phase B. She then told us some information that would not go public until the following day. The builder was dropping the purchase price of the home by almost $80,000 just to get it sold. Not $10,000. Not even $25,000. Dropping the price by almost $80,000. At that price point, we could get the house and still live. We told the representative we would be in the next day to put down earnest money and sign some paperwork. If the price drop wasn't enough to say this was a "God thing" that David and I got this house, then the fact that another couple went to the model home that very weekend and offered full price for the house we had been looking at was proof enough. But David and I already had the contract. That's God.

There was a month's difference between the closing date on the sale of our old house and the closing date on our new house. Yay! Yes. Fun? No. David and I, along with some wonderful friends, moved everything we owned into storage for a month. Yes, we had to rent a storage facility and live at a hotel for a month. Sofia and Lily thought staying at a hotel was an adventure. They loved jumping from bed to bed, and the hotel had a pool and free breakfast every morning. We all had some fun, humorous moments, but the entire situation was a major juggling act for David and me. But we were not complaining. We were moving. We got a brand-new house and another new beginning. I really did believe this was the break we had been needing and the answer to many of our problems.

Once we were all moved into our new home, we began experiencing new issues. Sofia and Lily had never lived in a two-story home, and they were afraid to sleep upstairs. The master bedroom was on the main floor. David and I had to buy chairs that folded out into twin beds for the girls to sleep downstairs in the living room. I realize some people may say that David and I brought many issues upon ourselves by not setting more guidelines at home. I get that. But when you have children who hardly sleep and are afraid to be alone, you do whatever is necessary to ensure some peace and sleep in the home. Keep in mind, we were still having serious issues going on with Lily. I do not over-exaggerate when I say she had a meltdown every single night from one to two hours long…screaming, crying, throwing stuff, hitting, knocking furniture over, scratching herself, or banging her head against the wall. David and I had to watch her to make sure she didn't hurt herself. You never knew what would set her off, and she never remembered the episode afterward. Sometimes I would gently blow in her face, and that had a calming effect on her. Sometimes you could pick her up if she wasn't flailing and walk around with her until she came down from her outrage. And there were times absolutely nothing would soothe her. You could ask her questions about what upset her afterward, and she did not have a clue. And Lily sincerely felt sorry for her actions once she had regained her composure.

I acquired some recommendations on pediatricians near our new home. The doctor we started taking the girls to was highly recommended, but the next couple of years with her were so disheartening. David and I tried and tried to get this new doctor to test Lily to try and find out what was wrong with her. The doctor would belittle David and me, tell us it was just tantrums and to just step over Lily and let her have her fits. She even told us we just weren't very good parents if we couldn't handle a toddler. We were told Lily would grow out of it. Well, she wasn't growing out of it, and the "Hulk Smashes" continued to get worse. She was getting bigger and hitting harder, throwing furniture and endless screaming. We had asked many other parents if they had any similar experiences, but they all said no and that it was probably something she would grow out of. David and I knew that people were genuinely trying to help, but it was hard hearing that phrase when Lily was not growing out of it. We did not know where to turn. It was frustrating that doctors would not even take the magnitude of the issue with Lily seriously.

When Lily started kindergarten at the local elementary, David and I were praying for the best. Lily got in trouble constantly and had notes sent home almost daily. She was smart, but she caused disruptions in the classroom and could not sit still. Once she was finished with her work, she decided she needed to assist the other children with their work. This was not welcomed by the teacher, of course. By the end of the school year, the teacher asked to meet with David and me and suggested that we hold Lily back for another year of kindergarten. David and I were like, "Absolutely not." Lily made good grades; she just could not focus and be still. David and I then decided to give her the summer to develop, mature, and receive tutoring, and if she did poorly in first grade, we would hold her back a year. This was so hard for us.

But there was a silver lining. Lily was due to go in for her yearly check-up. These appointments were never fun. I would get to hear what terrible parents we were once again from the doctor. Lily had gotten so bad with the nightly meltdowns that some nights David and I would just go sit on the front porch until she calmed down. I know that sounds horrible, but Lily would scream so loud that you could hear her outside. We honestly told Sofia that if the police ever showed up at our house, she was our only alibi that we were not abusing Lily because it sounded like it with all her screaming. Lily was completely uncontrollable when she had these meltdowns.

To my wonderful surprise, Lily's normal pediatrician was no longer with the practice, so we were oh-so blessed to see a new doctor. Dr. Harston was a Godsend. Even before the end of the appointment, she looked at me, pointed at Lily, and asked, "Is she always like this?" Lily was trying to open locked drawers, pulling out all the children's books, climbing on stuff, and just going non-stop. I told the doctor, "Oh, this is calm for her." I went on to tell her about everything that had happened with Lily from the time we adopted her and that the previous doctor accused us of everything, including being bad parents for letting our child act the way she did. I went on to explain that Lily really was an incredible child. She was smart. She was very loving. She was helpful. She just could not sit still. She was into everything. She was destructive. I further explained that Lily would behave pretty well until later in the day when she would have a daily meltdown of screaming, crying, hurting herself and others. I told the doctor David and I were at our wits' end because we did not know how to help our daughter, and it was affecting the entire household.

Dr. Harston suggested we have Lily tested for ADHD because she clearly showed all the signs of it. ADHD? What? Really? Yes? Okay, David and I were willing to try anything. And thank God a doctor finally listened and believed there was an issue. Wow. Was this really happening? Amen!

David and I were able to have Lily tested over the summer between her kindergarten year and 1st grade year. When we received the results, the breath was knocked out of me, and I teared up. David started reading the diagnosis that was sent to us. We went in for one possible diagnosis and received five different diagnoses. Lily did indeed have ADHD, as Dr. Harston suspected, but that wasn't all we would be dealing with.

Before I go into that, another transition was going on in our lives. The community we were now living in was organizing a church within the community. David and I were still driving back across town to attend our church, where David was Associate Pastor. I asked David if he would mind if I went to one of the informational meetings about this new church. He said he didn't mind, but he did not have any plans on leaving our church. I went to the meeting and was very interested. I thought the way the church was being set up was a little strange. Instead of one specific senior pastor, there was going to be three. Well, two men and a couple that would rotate on leading church services. I met the youth pastor and altogether kind of liked the idea of the plan this church had. I attended the church on the second Sunday that they were open and had service. The church was small, still getting organized, but I liked it.

One of the pastors at the church within our community was British, and he invited David and me to his house for tea and biscuits one afternoon. For non-British folks, biscuits are cookies. I just thought I'd throw that in there. David and I were always ready to meet people in the neighborhood and make new friends. We were surprised when one of the other pastors and his wife were there as well. To make a very long story short, they expressed to us that they were looking for a fourth pastor to help lead the church. These men had heard about David through people in the community that knew

David was a pastor. David had prayed for people and helped out if there was a need within the community. The other pastors we were visiting with felt like David was already pastoring the neighborhood and asked him to join the leadership. David and I were like, "We just came over here for tea and biscuits." We thanked them for the offer and agreed to pray about it and get back to them. This totally came out of left field, I assure you.

David and I talked about the offer and prayed about it. When I had first mentioned moving from Rockwall to Arlington, David had been against the suggestion, but at this point, he was glad that we did move. When I first mentioned the possibility of attending this new church, David was okay with me visiting but expected nothing more. Then this job offer was just dropped in his lap. David wouldn't get paid, but he would be part of church leadership in our own community. It would also be great for our kids to grow and expand during this new season in our lives. Sofia and Lily could not be actively involved at the church we were attending at the time because of the distance. David was hesitant at first, but with the laborious traveling we had to do driving back across town for church, it just made sense. We were all in.

Earlier I mentioned that some people were not so happy that David and I were moving to Arlington. Well, after certain individuals found out we were leaving the church David had attended since he was a boy, I found out just how some of the people at our church really felt about me. Although most of the congregation was genuinely nice to me, David and I knew there was some apprehension where I was concerned ever since we got married. Now, remember, I was completely honest in pre-marital counseling and let it be known that I did not want to take on a ministry role at the church, but I would support David. We were told that nothing more would be expected of me. But evidently, this was not accurate. It was during this time I found out that I had been expected to take over the women's ministry at some point, although no one ever conveyed that to me at any point in time. It was said of me that I was pulling David away from his calling. His calling was to serve, and he would still be doing that. But the biggest slap in the face was that the senior pastor himself told David that, "If it wasn't for Julie, I would have made you Senior Pastor years ago." What? This made David mad. David and I had decided to move and start a new life and help build a new church, but for some reason, I was being viciously attacked. I was a little lost at this point.

If you had any idea at all about what I had gone through over the years with certain individuals at this church, mainly knowing that they would tell me they loved me to my face then talk about me behind my back, you would wonder why we didn't leave sooner. But when I heard the accusations about myself from David, I didn't even flinch. I was not mad. I was not hurt. And I was not the least bit surprised. They needed a scapegoat, and I was the perfect one. The bottom line was that David made a decision for himself based on his family's needs and people were not happy about it. David was no longer chasing after the promise of full-time ministry at this church. He was moving on. Our departure was not accepted well, and we were treated very poorly. But we were not angry. We did not burn any bridges. We stepped down graciously. We were just ready to move on and get some much-needed family time back in our lives. No more commuting.

The previous several years of our lives consisted of much chaos surrounding us. There were a lot of good memories. There were a lot of bad memories. But with our new situation, not only did we have a new home near our work, but we were also making new friends, David was going to start fulfilling a lifelong dream of helping to lead a church, and we finally found out what was going on with our sweet yet emotional Lily.

We are not promised a life of ease. There are times that we are tested to the extreme of our limitations. I do not know what loss you may have experienced. I have no idea what struggles you have come up against. I haven't a clue about the thoughts that infiltrate your mind. But as you have read, I have been let down, abused, judged, broken, and much more. If I have learned anything in life, I have learned to fight. Most of my fights take place on my knees. There are so many things that are out of our control. But we always have a choice on how we respond to challenges. My responses have not always been the right ones. I have learned that there are just some things that all I can do is pray about and give it over to God. There are other times that I have to make changes in my life. But in the end, my trust is in God. Never give up. You are worth the fight. Don't stop. Don't give in. Keep moving forward. Believe.

"Raise A Hallelujah"

-By: Bethel Music with Johnathan David and Melissa Helser

Chapter 11

Tangled Emotions
Help Is On The Way

As David read the letter that contained Lily's diagnosis, we were astonished. We just wanted to know if she had ADHD or not. Lily's test confirmed ADHD, but the letter went on to say that Lily also had ODD. Goodness, we had no idea. David and I had never even heard of ODD. We had to look that one up. Oppositional Defiant Disorder. This disorder causes one to be aggressive, defiant, and disobedient. One might be irritable as well. The more David and I read, the more we felt like ODD sounded exactly like Lily's behavior patterns. The cause of ODD is not known, but some would say the disorder deals with a combination of genetic and environmental factors. Combine ODD with ADHD, and the diagnosis completely explained Lily's behavior. The therapist also concluded that Lily had signs of depression and anxiety and suffered from abandonment issues, probably due to being given up for adoption.

David and I just sat there. Numb. Sober. Then we thanked God. After all these years of not knowing what was wrong with our daughter or how to help her, we now had a place to start with seeking help. Thank God. When we explained Lily's diagnosis to her, she seemed relieved as well. She had not known what would cause her to have emotional meltdowns, and she always felt horrible about the way she acted afterward. We had hope. She had hope. Sofia was relieved as well.

In the following months, David and I were able to get Lily on ADHD medication and found her a therapist. Lily became a completely different, happy, calm child. I am not exaggerating. It was an immediate difference in her. The first day she was on her ADHD medication, Sofia came into the living room and did a double-take. Lily was watching a movie, sitting still, quiet, laughing. Lily had never been able to sit down and watch an entire movie previously. She could not sit still and focus. Sofia just looked at me and pointed at Lily, and I was like, "I know, right?" Another positive aspect was that Lily now understood her condition. She had felt like she was just a bad girl, and now she knew that her brain was different and that the things she did were not her fault. Lily also knew that she was better now. The hulk smashes meltdowns stopped. She no longer hurt herself or anyone else in the house. Lily's medical condition was under control. It was a lot for a child so young to realize and comprehend, but she got it. Lily's life completely changed. Our entire household changed for the better. We all felt like we could breathe again. Our daily routine no longer consisted of waiting for Lily's next episode. She was just her sweet, loving self. The irregularities in her brain were now being regulated by medication. Lily was happy. David, Sofia, and I were overjoyed. The years of emotional tension and chaos were over. Thank God, again and again.

Lily was later diagnosed with dyslexia as well. She has had to take part in special classes to help her in that area, but Lily is giving her all in order to power through the educational setbacks associated with dyslexia. I always tell her that she is my hero because no matter what life throws at her, she finds a way to rise above and not let her disabilities label her or hold her back. Yes, Lily is pretty awesome.

During this time…I know I keep saying that, but there was always something else going on…Sofia had an emotional breakdown. It took place during her 5th grade year. She had always been a very outgoing, happy, full-of-life young girl. When Sofia was a very little girl, she could not pronounce her name, so if you asked her what her name was, she would reply, "Sassy." Sassy sounds close enough to Sofia. The name stuck, and she was our "Sassy-pants." Sofia was not at all sassy. On the contrary, she was sweet. I believe that Sofia began to withdraw because of the tension associated with the years that Lily went undiagnosed correctly, along with the other issues David and I were having. She was still a very spirited young girl, but she wasn't herself. Maybe David and I had missed something. We had thought that life was better at home once Lily was on medication. We were wrong.

Suddenly something happened one day. David and I just weren't sure what happened. Sofia and Lily had been on Christmas break for two weeks. When the girls were released from school for Christmas break, Sofia was fine. The day I took her back to school, she wasn't fine. As Sofia and I were sitting in the drop-off lane at school, Sofia started shaking. I assumed she was a little nervous about returning to school, but when I asked her what was wrong, she started trembling and crying and told me she couldn't get out of the car. Sofia then added she couldn't go into the school. As a mom, the first questions I asked were, "Did something happen at school? Did someone touch you?" I also asked about bullying because she had been bullied before. Sofia couldn't even answer me. She was just crying and again stated she could not get out of the car. Someone approached the car to open her door, and she freaked out. I pulled forward, and I called David. He said to take her home, and we could call the school and say she was sick. David and I tried but could not get any answers out of Sofia. She didn't have any answers. She had no clue what was causing this sudden fear.

The next day, the same thing happened. Sofia got up and got ready, and when we got to the school, she started crying and trembling again and said she couldn't get out of the car. I called David, and he said to bring her to work, and he would take her to school and talk to the office and teachers. Over the following days, the faculty was extremely helpful. One teacher suggested Sofia print a big picture of her family and put it in the front of her binder so if she got scared, she could see her family and know she was okay. There were days David would get called to the school because Sofia was having a breakdown. Other days I would go to her school during lunch and have lunch with her to make sure she was emotionally functioning well. We did whatever we could to ease her fear and help her manage being at school.

David and I asked if she was open to seeing a therapist. Sofia was fine with that suggestion. She wanted to know what the issue was with her as much as we did. Sofia was diagnosed with Social Anxiety Disorder. We have no idea what caused the onset of this disorder or why it came on so suddenly and so strong. But now, we had something to work with, a diagnosis.

Sofia took part in several therapy sessions that seemed to help her deal with her disorder. Then, to our surprise and relief, as quickly as Social Anxiety Disorder came upon Sofia, it was gone. Or was it? Sofia seemed to be completely back to her old self until Spring 2020. For four years, it seemed as though Social Anxiety Disorder was a thing in Sofia's past. When Spring Break took place in 2020, and the girls did not return to school due to Covid, Sofia's anxiety crept back into her life. She was prescribed anti-anxiety medication, which has helped Sofia to keep calm. She also returned to therapy and has learned techniques to help her work through her fears. But even today, Sofia continues to deal with anxiety. She is strong, and she is persevering.

It is agonizing to see your children suffer emotionally and feel as though you can do nothing to help them. Our home life was turned completely upside down prior to Lily being diagnosed with ADHD, ODD, anxiety, depression, and abandonment issues. Sofia's Social Anxiety Disorder was seemingly short-lived, but it was never really gone.

Anxiety is a challenging emotional disorder to deal with. I want to further explain both Lily's and Sofia's emotional breakdowns in case you know anyone that may be showing similar behavior patterns. Lily would bite, pull wads of hair from Sofia's head, pinch, throw things, turn furniture over, move furniture away from the wall. She was only two or three when she started doing these things. When Lily had hulk smashes, she had strength that was unbelievable. She would scratch herself, scratch furniture, bang her head against the wall, punch herself in the face. Yes. Lily would also scratch and hit Sofia and David. She punched David in the throat one time and kicked him where no man wants to be kicked. The only time she kicked me was when I was pulling her off someone else or picking her up off the ground and trying to calm her or take her to her room. No one else ever saw her act out like this. We saw it every single day. I had to film Lily with my phone in order to show Lily's pediatrician and therapist. I asked why Lily only acted out at home. David and I were told because it was her safe place. Lily knew she could allow her bottled-up emotions explode at home. I have had multiple people tell me this same information.

Then let us look at Sofia. Her anxiety turns her into a trembling youth that to this day always has a bowl and crackers in her room because her stomach churns much of the time. She feels sick when anxiety hits her. I cannot remember how many times she has had to be picked up early from school. Lily is my cuddle bear. Sofia is a normal don't-hug-on-me teenager. So, it is not normal when my 15-year-old has asked me to sleep in her room with her because she is afraid she might die in the middle of the night. ADHD is real. ODD is real. Anxiety and depression are real. Abandonment issues are real. What I want to convey here is that if you notice any unusual behavior in your children, please do not simply dismiss their behavior or label them as "bad kids." And don't assume it must be hormones or something similar. There is no shame in having your children tested for something, for anything.

If a child's behavior is unusual, aggressive, fearful, or "off" in any way, there is most likely an underlying reason. Seek help. Ask questions. Start with a school counselor if you are unsure of where to begin. If your child needs to be administered medication or go to therapy, there is no shame in either of these means of treatment. Lily's life was entirely transformed once we received her diagnosis and were able to take the necessary steps to help her function normally. Sofia was overcome by fear and needed professional help in order to manage that issue. I cringe to think how many children go undiagnosed and are suffering in life. There are times in life we all need help. Our emotions can be beautiful. Our emotions can be destructive. I am not talking about only children here. If you behave in a way that distresses you, please do not believe the lie, "that's just the way you are." Wrong. Every emotional issue has a root. And that root needs to be dug up and dealt with. I will go deeper into that when I discuss EMDR Therapy. Never allow doubt or fear to paralyze you. Pray. Seek help. Have someone to stand with you in life's battles. Hope is a power within itself.

Chapter 12

Alone
Never Alone

When I moved back to Texas from Nashville, I really was starting from scratch. I was moving to the huge Dallas-Fort Worth Metroplex, where I knew absolutely no one. I started my new job. I would still be working in television, but the work I would be doing was totally different from anything I had done before. I had met some ladies at work, and they were amazing, but I did not really have time to meet and make new close friends. But then I met David, so I thought I was alright. I would like to stress the importance of friendships. I had about 30 people that I ran around with in Nashville, and when I moved back to Texas, I had no one. Or at least that was how it felt. My family was two hours away from me, and I visited them often, but the people I was meeting already had their friendship circles. I was still settling into my new apartment and new job, but I was missing my friends in Nashville. I felt very alone. Always remember that your feelings will lie to you because this issue of feeling alone became a big issue.

David and I had struggles in our marriage from day one. I realize that every marriage has challenges or valleys. It just seemed like it was one thing after another with us, though. We spent the first three years of our marriage paying off debt from his first marriage. This situation was not his fault, and I was aware of the financial issues before I married David. We were able to eventually get everything paid off. Then the fertility issues hit, and all that happened through that. Add adoption. Difficulties. Diagnosis. What these things were causing. Distance. Hurt feelings. Feeling worn. Then David's mom did pass away from cancer. David had lost most of his family in about three years…dad, brother, mom. The stress and tension in our home continued to mount. David and I were not intending to grow apart, but it was happening.

Although Joyce and I had our ups and downs over the years, we were family, and she loved our daughters, and that was enough for me. Joyce was the best grandmother any kid could have ever wished for. Her death was a hard blow. It was during summer break, and David had just dropped Sofia and Lily off at Vacation Bible School. He was on his way to the hospital to visit his mom when his sister called and told him to get there fast. David was able to get to the hospital in time to say goodbye, which meant the world to him. He called me and asked me to get to the hospital as soon as possible. There were other family members bringing Sofia and Lily to the hospital, but David did not want the girls to see their adored grandmother lifeless in her hospital bed. Joyce was a proud Pentecostal woman. She hated losing her hair to the cancer treatments. She took great pride in always looking so put together and with her hair up in a bun. Before I left her room to get Sofia and Lily, I bent over, kissed her on the cheek, and told her she looked beautiful. And she did. She looked completely peaceful as well. Joyce had never been the same since Thomas died. She always said a parent should never have to bury a child. I agree. We knew she was happy to be at home in heaven with Tom, Thomas, and all their dogs.

I knew the loss of Joyce would hit David hard. My heart broke for him. I still had my entire family. I had no idea what he was going through. David had gotten to talk to his mom the day before she passed. I think she knew her time in this world was coming to an end. She was sharing information and thoughts with David. I wish David had not shared one of their last conversations with me. But he needed to talk, and I listened. I really thought she had gotten over David marrying me. All these years, there was a little tension between us, but we were nice to each other, we laughed, and we ate and prayed together. But one of the last things she said to David was, "Don't let that Baptist girl get you out of church." I didn't need to hear that. It hurt. I'd already been accused of pulling him away from his calling at our previous church. Once again, I was being judged for things I hadn't even done. I was being shamed. I had dealt with this issue most of my life, and I just couldn't kick it. And since shame tells you that you are something wrong, I believe I became more and more of an introvert. That wasn't who I was. I was quite the opposite. But I had allowed the difficulties and judgments of others to really make me go into that walled-up mode again. I was tired of people hurting me for absolutely no reason other than because of who I was. I often thought to myself, "What is wrong with me?"

Several years ago, my mom shared something with me that is, even today, priceless to me. When I was a little girl, and we lived next door to my dad's parents, I was constantly running across the field to go to Nannie and Granddaddy's house. I loved being there. I felt special there. It was one of my favorite places to be. My mom told me that one day I came home and asked her a question. I don't remember this, but mom said I looked at her and asked, "Do you know why I like going to Nannie's so much? Because she lets me just be me." That's powerful.

Although we all know that we are never alone because God is always with us, the emotion of feeling alone can be overwhelmingly depleting. How was it that I felt so alone? I work for a television show that raises money to drill water wells, build orphanages, provide feeding programs, rescues women and children out of sex trafficking, provides cleft palate and club foot surgeries all around the world, and takes the knowledge of a loving God to millions of people in need all over the world. I was at a church that my husband was helping to lead. I absolutely love being a mom, but I had few friends. I knew a whole lot of people. But knowing people and having close friendships are two different things. I had a couple of girlfriends, but David and I lived such busy lives. David and I saw other families going on vacations, having parties, and so much more, but we just could not seem to get our lives in order. We were functioning, but there was always something that kept us from really living. We always felt just outside of where we wanted to be in life. David and I either didn't have the time or the money to go on dates. And I realize now that situation was totally our fault. We did not prioritize us. But when you are just trying to survive until the next day, you make wrong decisions.

This whole thought of feeling alone will come into play again when I talk about EMDR Therapy. But in the meantime, our marriage was falling apart. I am leaving out many details but just know that most people we knew thought we were the perfect couple. We weren't. I am telling you that I cannot even begin to explain or make you realize how much I prayed and fasted for my marriage. I am sure David prayed as well. But we weren't praying together, and we continued to grow apart. There were issues at home. Major issues. For years we had one struggle after another. Again, David was a very broken person when we got married. I was a very broken person when we got married. Two broken pieces do not make a whole.

"...healthy marriages can only be made between two healthy people... personal pain or brokenness or struggle leads to pain and brokenness and struggle in our marriage. Marriage is like so many other things: we get out of it what we put into it."

--Shauna Niequist, Author and Speaker

I suggested counseling again, but David was not interested. I went to counseling for a time, but this therapist just was not helping me or shedding any light on David's and my situation, so I quit going. There was one major issue that plagued David and me throughout our entire marriage, and it was getting worse. Whenever I brought it up, he would deny it or just say we saw things differently. I felt like we were fighting a losing battle, and our marriage was going down in the muck and mire of a littered battlefield. Why wasn't God answering my prayers and saving our marriage? For years, I prayed for David to change. That was wrong. I admit it. Then for years, I prayed for God to change me. Then I just started praying, "Do something, God! Please!" Many nights I went to sleep crying. How did we get to this place?

Then I thought maybe it's just me. I had been a screw-up since day one. My mom once told me she never wanted four kids, but that dad said they would not stop having kids until they had a girl. My mom said she was very happy when I came along. But how do you think it makes a person feel when your mother says she never wanted four kids and you were the fourth? Unwanted? A mistake? Like your very existence is "wrong"? I will point out that my mother said this to me when she was "medicating," and she does not recall saying it to me. I am no longer hurt by it and have a better understanding of my mother.

I am a God-loving, Jesus-praising, Holy-Spirit-filled, praying, fasting, church-going woman of God, full of faith. But I was also battle weary. And one thing after another in my life made me feel very unworthy and unloved. Again, I do not want to make it sound like every single day of my life was miserable, life sucked, and there were never any fun times and happiness. That would be a complete lie. David and I had many wonderful, special times together, and we had many more laughs and good times when we became parents. I just need to acknowledge the persistent assaults on David, me, our family, and our marriage. The enemy does not play fair. Even so, with the magnitude of problems we faced, God was there with us, even if we might not have felt His presence at times.

Counseling did not help me. I was grasping for anything that I thought might help me. My friend Susan, who went to Gateway Church at the time, told me about a conference her church held every year. It was called the *Kairos Conference*. I read up on it, and it sounded amazing. I needed help. God wasn't talking to me (so I thought), so I was going to take off work and go to this two-day conference and hopefully get some much-needed answers that I was searching for. Upon arrival at Gateway Church, I noticed there were probably a couple thousand people attending this conference. I picked up my Kairos packet and went and found a seat. The event began with praise and worship, which I needed to set the mood and prepare me to receive anything God had for me. I felt desperate. I needed God to show up.

I will just say that it was an amazing two-day event. I took pages and pages of notes. I listened intently to all the wonderful and gifted speakers. I was so glad that I went. But there was one thing that happened that made me know why I was at that conference…why I felt led to register and attend. At one point, there was a speaker that spoke on parent wounds. Many issues that people have today can be traced back to something that had to do with one or both of their parents.

At the end of that session, volunteers spread out across the front of the stage. The speaker compassionately said, "If you have a parent wound, there are people here at the front that are here to pray for you, give you a hug, or whatever you need." There was a man that looked very much like my dad. Tall. Slender. Graying, thinning hair. I decided I wanted a hug from him. I wanted to imagine my dad hugging me as this lookalike man was hugging me. Evidently, he looked like a lot of other people's dads because he had a long line waiting to get a hug from him…great for him for God to use him in that way.

But I was disappointed. Why? I don't know. Maybe I wanted to see if something "magical" would happen, and all the wounds of my past would fade away and finally be healed. Every time I thought I had a breakthrough; shame would arise once more and reveal my bruised heart and broken mind. And it would make me feel like dirt. But I was already in the aisle at Gateway Church, so I just went up and let another man hug me. I had checked out by then because I couldn't get to the gentleman that I wanted a hug from. Mature of me? Of course not. But, as always, God had gone before me and had a plan in the works.

The sanctuary was dim, low music was playing, people were experiencing healing, and I was heading back to my seat. Suddenly an arm reached through the dark and pulled me over to a seat. A woman was standing there, and she looked into my eyes. She had tears in her eyes as she spoke these words to me, "I don't know what you went down front for, but I watched you every step of the way. And as you were walking back to your seat, God told me to tell you that you are not alone."

I froze because I was captivated by what she said. This time I did not freeze in fear. I froze in astonishment. God saw me. He had a stranger speak what I hadn't been willing to hear on my own. I knew God loved me and heard my prayers. But many times, I felt invisible to God or that He had forgotten about me. Although that is never true. God knew what I needed at that exact moment in time. Reassurance. Affirmation of His love for me. I felt warm all over. I thanked the lady for being obedient to God's prompting and slowly made my way back to my seat. God made a point to get my attention in this area. It was a special moment. It was the beginning of something in me. I didn't know it then, but God was beginning to unveil and unravel something that had tormented me my entire life.

If you are in a season of your life where you feel alone, forgotten, invisible, unimportant, lost, far from the person you want to be, stop and refocus. There are times in my life when I notice my thoughts going down a negative road, and I start believing the lies in my head. But then I would stop and count backward from five. 5...4...3...2...1. This brief five seconds can allow you to refocus your negative thought process and turn it around. Motivational speaker Mel Robbins wrote a book about this technique called "The 5 Second Rule." I have not read her book but I heard Mel speak about it. Mel expresses her belief that this simple rule can help you break any bad habit. With me, it helps me to refocus. Do not allow your thoughts to keep you in a dark place and feeling alone when you were meant to shine. You are never alone. God reassured me of that during the conference through that woman, but He later even made it clearer to me.

"You're Not Alone"

-By: Meredith Andrews

Chapter 13

Downward Spiral: Feelings of Betrayal
Upward Climb: Looking Beyond Ourselves

I was on a spiritual and emotional "high" after the conference. But what I experienced at this event did not change the atmosphere at home. I mean, I shared the encounter with the woman and what God spoke to me through her with David, and he was thrilled for me. He had always thought I was a little messed up from my past, and I had always thought he was a little messed up from his. I assure you that I do not say this out of disrespect. Truth is truth, and David and I were both very aware of each other's pasts prior to getting married. What we did not know was that there were much deeper issues that we could not have even realized…issues that would somewhat sabotage areas of our lives and lead to bad choices.

David truly was my best friend. Sure, we each had our share of "baggage" and stumbling blocks to overcome, but most people do. I knew I could go to him for prayer. If I was sick, he would help take care of me. He helped provide for our family. We were there for each other through all the hurdles life placed in front of us. The issues that over-shadowed us just drove us further and further apart with each passing year. David and I had love for each other, but we were going nowhere. Our marriage relationship had been unimaginably put to the test time and time again over the years. David and I were worn, tired, and drifting apart. But we had a family and responsibilities, so we did what many people who are hurting and needing help do…we painted on our happy faces in public and moved forward.

Our issues had become bigger than us. By now, David and I were pretty much living as roommates. We did not go on dates. There was no affection between us. I believe we were both in survival mode and running on empty. There were pre-existing issues within this new church that we had not been made aware of prior to David accepting the position. There were predicaments taking place that left me feeling uneasy. And I felt like I was having to keep secrets again, which did not sit well with me. Decisions were being made regarding this new church that I felt like I was left out of. It was a hard season. Everything in David's and my life seemed to be falling apart. Over the years, David had become more and more angry, aggressive, and spent more and more time involved in ministry work and withdrawn. Over the years, I had become more hurt, bitter, resentful, and withdrawn. We tried to work around our issues. Well, you don't work around issues. You kill them, or they kill your marriage. David and I just could not resolve our battles. I could not go on with the charade any longer.

Call me selfish. Call me weak. Trust me; I had called myself those things for years. But I had prayed and suggested counseling for years. I had told David he was going to push me too far one day, and when he did, I was done. Well, I was done. We weren't happy. We were each doing life on our own. He spent his free time involved in church stuff and people. I spent my free time at the gym. In the evenings, we pulled it all together for Sofia and Lily. It was no longer a marriage. And if we weren't going to counseling for the desperate help that we needed, it was obvious we were going nowhere.

I hope you do not stop reading here. I realize that I am not painting a very good picture of myself here. But I must allow you to see how bad things had gotten, how low David and I had gone. I am just being as real and honest as I can be with this part of the story so you will realize the depth of despair that I had plunged into and how my mind was being twisted. Don't give up on me here. There is a beautiful redemption story before this is all over.

I took a day off work and went to see a lawyer. I was just so tired of us hurting each other. David and I were probably both being selfish. I don't think either of us really knew what to do anymore. So, I did it. I filed for divorce in 2017. I was afraid to tell David that I had filed for divorce. I did not know how he would react. I knew I did not want to discuss a divorce with Sofia and Lily around. Now, please do not think that I am throwing David under the bus. I didn't like him much anymore, but I didn't like me either. We cared about each other's well-being. We did not want anything bad to happen to the other person. But we really were not a part of each other's lives anymore. We lived in the same house. We were both helping to raise our children. We looked good to the outside world. But we were not living as a married couple anymore. We truly had not been for years. If our pasts weren't enough, we had allowed "life" to turn us into people we weren't. And all this happened while we were living for God and serving in ministry. Satan doesn't take breaks. He will attack you whenever and wherever he can.

One day I asked David to go to a park near our house. I did not know how to tell him I had filed for divorce. Believe it or not, I did not want to hurt him. We had hurt each other enough. I never believed on the day we said, "I do," that we would end up in such a broken state. I finally just spit it out, "I filed for divorce." He just looked at me and said, "No." I told him about my meeting with the lawyer. I told him that I would not have him served papers at work. We both worked at the same company, and I would never want to do something to embarrass him like that.

It was not a comfortable situation for either of us, as you can imagine. The thing that I didn't understand, though, was that he acted like I blindsided him. I expressed how we didn't even live like a married couple anymore and how everyone walked on eggshells in our home. That was not marriage. That was not family. It was merely existing and living a lie. I couldn't do that anymore.

David asked me to put the divorce on pause. I asked him, "Why, what is going to change?" He said he would go to counseling. He said he would do what he had to do as long as I would not divorce him. He stated his first marriage had failed and that he could not go through that again.

I honestly did not know what to do. I did not know what I felt. But David was finally willing to go to counseling, so he deserved that chance. David immediately found a counselor. He started going to therapy. David continued counseling for a few months. The therapist concluded that David had never mourned the deaths of his dad, brother, and mom. The therapist added that due to the factor that David's pain and loss had never been dealt with, his hurt was coming out as anger.

That made perfect sense to me. But did it erase all that had happened within our marriage and household the past few years? David had become an angry and self-focused person, even though he thought very little of himself because of the brokenness in his past. I had become a very distant and self-focused person, even though I thought very little of myself due to my past. I believe traumatic experiences had flooded our abilities to even realize how our pasts had shaped us. And I am not just talking about the past as our childhoods and teens years. Our adult years had wreaked havoc on us as well. Although we lived lives of serving and ministry, we could not fix what was right in front of us.

The divorce was on pause, and in the following year or so, David and I tried. At least, I think we would both say we tried. I just believe the damage had been done. Nothing is impossible or beyond repair. We had already seen God work miracles in our children's lives, but I honestly think we both checked out. David might not agree with that, but the same issues kept coming up. And remember, there is so much that I am not sharing simply due to time. But David and I were back in the same depleting rut. On top of our own personal issues, I felt as though David and I were setting a poor example of what a marriage should look like for our girls. David and I were not affectionate. We did not even sleep in the same room. He snores. I am a light sleeper. He tried a sleep study. I tried prescription and over-the-counter sleeping pills and earplugs. Our schedules were constantly packed. There were just miles and distance between us. It broke my heart. And I know it broke his.

I have intentionally left out what I am about to discuss until now. Not because it still affects or hurts me. But because it is a delicate matter. In an earlier chapter, I mentioned that one issue plagued David and me throughout our entire marriage. David did not see it as problematic, but I did. Arguments often resulted when this subject was approached. In the simplest terms, I felt like David put ministry work before me, before our marriage, before our kids, before our family. I felt like we got what was left of him. I once told David that ministry was "the other woman" to me, and I could not compete. That may sound absurd, but if you have never experienced something like this, you probably could not easily understand. I felt as though everyone else's needs were more important than my needs and the needs of Sofia and Lily.

Now, one might say that I knew what I was getting into when I married a pastor. Yes and no. David was a youth pastor when we married, and I wasn't expecting him to basically be working two full-time jobs, one as a television editor and one as a pastor. I also did not know that we would spend 12 years commuting on average three hours a day while David was working all these hours. I'm sure my abandonment issues played into my feelings of betrayal, but I felt as though David poured more of himself into the needs of the church than into his family. The reason I share this briefly is to lay the background for what I am about to share.

Then it happened. Through a series of events and even some decisions that I did not agree with and was pretty much left out of, our marriage came to a final crossroads. David made a decision that I was totally against. He was offered the position of Senior Pastor at our church. I expressed to him, "I don't think this is a good idea. Our marriage is falling apart, and we need to work on us." He looked at me and said, "I've waited for an opportunity like this all my life, and I'm gonna take it. God will take care of us." At that moment, I felt like I did not matter, our family did not matter, our marriage was not a partnership, and that I had no say or input on what was best for our future. Now don't throw stones at David. As horrible as this was for me at the time, looking back, I think I have a better understanding of this situation, and I will explain later.

After the shock of this decision, I tried to be happy and supportive of it, but I just felt betrayed and like an outsider in my own marriage. I was in many ways happy for David, but I no longer saw an "us." I honestly don't know if I had for a long time. The distance between us grew. We hung in there but was it even for the right reasons anymore? Prayers and fasting didn't seem to be changing anything or anyone, David or me. I am just being honest. I was no longer filling his cup. He was no longer filling mine. It just seemed like we were no longer what each other needed. And we were both looking for someone to blame. Maybe this all sounds like a cop-out, but it is the truth of where we were in life.

So, in 2019, I took the "pause" off the divorce. When I called my lawyer, she told me that it had been about a year, and she was getting ready to contact me to see if the file needed to be closed. I told her I would come to her office and meet with her and set things in motion. The marriage was over. It had been for years.

I met with David in our home and told him the divorce had been re-opened. This had been the third time in less than ten years that we had come to this point. It was a sad day, and many emotions were expressed. I told David that if he would just trust me, he could save a lot of money and not even bother getting a lawyer. I told him that I would be fair and that I would even let him read the draft of the divorce papers, and he could change anything he did not agree with before I had the final papers drawn up. Our marriage was not a marriage. It wasn't even a partnership. Neither of us was happy. It was time to acknowledge the obvious and deal with it at last.

Sofia and Lily were at friends' houses. David and I called them home. Sofia was 13, and Lily was 8 at the time. David and I sat them down and told them that I had filed for divorce. We explained a few things to them but left out facts that they did not need to know. Both girls handled the news very well. Children know more than we give them credit for. Lily teared up a little. She already had abandonment issues due to being given up for adoption. She needed more reassurance that everything was going to be okay. Sofia and Lily's biggest concern was that they loved our neighborhood and didn't want to leave. David and I promised the girls that we would work together to make every situation the best for everyone involved. In the end, David and I came up with a plan so that we could both remain living in our community. We asked the girls not to tell anyone about the divorce just yet. David and I had to figure out how we were going to handle this within the community, at church, and at our work since we worked together. We should have taken our own advice. He shared the news with church leadership, and we let our families and a few friends know. This proved to be a mistake on our part. Certain individuals immediately tried to pit David and me against each other. There were some people that got really ugly, really quick.

Divorce is never something anyone has on mind when you are standing in front of loved ones, in a beautiful dress or dashing suit, pledging to love till death do you part. Divorce is something that happens to other people. Right? Well, it happened to us. It was sad. It was hard. But just because David and my marriage did not work did not mean that all was lost. We still have the responsibility to co-parent and raise Sofia and Lily. We did not want our daughters to be statistics. We had to do this the right way for them.

Chapter 14

Divorce

Divorce sucks.

Chapter 15

Divorce and Dignity

David and I were both working for an international broadcast ministry. David was the pastor of a church. And we lived in a community with numerous friends that would undoubtingly be shocked as the news of our pending divorce was made public. In view of the fact that when David and I first shared the announcement with a few people, the response did not go well with certain individuals, and they tried to turn David and me against each other, we decided to keep the divorce private. Considering the divorce was going to be non-contested, we knew it could be finalized in about a period of two months. David and I continued to live in the same house. We did our best to prepare the children for the coming months. We both needed our jobs. Although David was Senior Pastor at his church, at the time he accepted the position, it was non-paying. At our television jobs, we decided we would wait to tell our bosses about the divorce in hopes that by the time the divorce was final, they would see that David and I were able to continue to work together without problems. Neither of us needed to lose our job. By no means do I want to make it sound like any of this was "easy," but David and I made a conscious decision that we wanted to make this transition as smooth as possible for Sofia and Lily. That meant David and I had to be at peace. And we were, at least in public and around the kids. I would be lying if I said there were no private heated discussions. This was hard on both of us.

I am not one to "air dirty laundry" on social media. I just believe some things are meant to be private. But, in the end, social media was the best way to relay the divorce information to everyone we knew all at one time. We did not want to have to tell the same story a few hundred times. It also allowed for a wall of protection while the news sunk in with everyone. I constructed a note to family and friends, David read and approved it, and this is what was posted on my Facebook page:

Divorce and Dignity

"As I write this, these words are so surreal because I write them from a place I never thought I would be: DIVORCED… or at least I will be next week. When I said, "I do," I meant it… forever. But sometimes "forever" isn't as long as we thought it would be.

I am not one to "air" my personal business on social media or publicly in any way, but I do feel led to write this, so there must be a reason.

Dignity is an admirable way of behaving.

The reason I titled this "Divorce & Dignity" is because I believe that trying or hard situations don't have to bring out the worst in people as it sometimes does. There are some people that will be in shock as they hear of the divorce of David and myself. I get it. I do. But I am writing this, with David's knowledge, so that we can get some information out that we want to share.

First of all, this is not an "easy" thing, but it is not an "ugly" thing either. David and I ask that our friends and family NOT "pick sides." David and I are still friends. David and I have two amazing children to raise. David and I will be showing up to a lot of the same events. We don't want anyone to feel uncomfortable. We don't. David and I will be living in the same neighborhood, just blocks away from each other, so Sofia and Lily can go back and forth between our house as they choose. I totally support David as the pastor of The Gathering Church.

The church has had a strong, positive impact on our kids, and Sofia and Lily want to continue to go there, so they will. I will pop in from time to time. No one needs to feel odd about that. David and I don't, so no one else should. We are still going to be a huge part of each other's lives, and we will continue to work together at our current job.

There has been give and take on both sides. There have been tears. There has been hurt. There has been honesty. There has been support. David's and my main goal right now is making this transition as good as possible for Sofia and Lily. They have known for months. They are aware of everything, and we talk openly about the situation.

For those who may ask "why" or "what happened," David and I will try to honor each other and keep things as private as we can. There are reasons or issues that led to this. We're not perfect. We are human. But what matters to us now is what happens from this point forward. We can't change the past, but we can try and make today and the future the best possible for all involved.

For those who may ask why we have not come forth with this information sooner, there is an easy answer. Early on, some people that knew tried to "pit" David and me against each other. We did not need that. Our kids did not need that. So, we made the decision to keep it pretty private until after the final papers were signed, and that happened this week, so we are making it public now.

For those who already knew, we thank you for your support and for continuing to love us both. David and I are still going to be part of each other's lives. We may not be married, but we have these two beautiful girls to raise, and we intend to do that to the best of our ability.

David will address this on Sunday at the church. But today... we are taking our girls out of town for the day for some rest and relaxation. Blessings to all."

That was in October of 2019. We sent out that message, turned our phones to silent, and drove out of town for the day. David's phone immediately started blowing up, but he ignored it. We wanted the girls to have a fun day. And we needed for all of us to leave the world behind for one day because we knew what and "who" (multiple people) we were about to have to face. I wish I could say that things went smoothly, but that would be far from the truth. I had no idea just how bad things would get. And I certainly had no idea just how immensely everything was going to affect me. I can only tell you what happened to me, from my point of view, and the impact it had on my life. But from the first impact, it was obvious that I was going to need counseling, so I quickly found a new psychologist.

Please know that David and I did not even divulge which one of us had filed for the divorce. A few people knew, but we did not think that anyone even needed to know that bit of information. We had hoped that withholding that information would allow people to see that we really were working together with all the aspects of the divorce. David even remained living with the girls and me for two months after the divorce until he could close on his new house and then move there. There was no point in David moving into an apartment for two months. This situation may have seemed odd to many, but we were trying to help each other out and ease into our new lives.

I will say that the following months of my life after the divorce were some of the most difficult I had ever gone through. Yes. Without a doubt. That statement speaks volumes, considering the trauma I had already been through. The divorce was final in October 2019. I assume I must have been naïve. I thought things would get better once David and I made it through the divorce. The situation was quite the opposite, and things got a bit nuts well into the following year.

Looking back now, it is currently a year and a half post-divorce, and all I can say is that I think something "snapped" in me. Whether it had to do with a culmination of the previous 35 years or so of my life or just the current situation I found myself in, I did not know at the time. But over the following months, several issues took place that brought out emotions in me that I didn't even know existed. That is what trauma does to you. You realize that what you thought you were in control of was in control of you. There was a period of about nine months after the divorce that I felt like I was losing my mind. But I can now say that those trials were a good thing. These situations made me face some demons in my life and finally put some things to rest.

I am only going to mention the things that were the most devastating to me and how they affected me, my emotions, and my mind. In a later chapter, I will share the root of all of these disastrous but defining moments in my life. Because, yes, there is a beautiful light at the end of the tunnel… but I had to go through much darkness and redemption to get there. Things were about to get ugly. Real ugly. Real fast.

Let's start with what happened when I did share the news of the impending divorce with my closest friend. I don't want to share her name, so I will call her Brooke. Brooke and I met at work and had been friends for well over ten years. David and I had agreed we could each tell our closest friend so we would each have someone to walk through the emotions of the divorce with us. I called Brooke into my office towards the end of the work-day, and she actually asked, "Are you and David getting divorced?" I told her, "Yes." Her reply was, "NO! If you and David can't make it, how on earth are we gonna make it?" She was referring to issues going on in her own marriage. Brooke was sad. She was hurt. She was upset. She asked questions. She had a lot to say. I thought that was it. It wasn't. Later Brooke texted me. She sent me a scathing text. I could not believe it. It knocked me back a few steps. Brooke told me that divorce was not biblical. She told me I was being selfish. She told me I was just doing this (divorce) because I was resentful for David's actions and I should give him another chance. She blasted me. I could not believe it. This was my closest friend. David and I kept our personal lives private, but we each had one friend that we shared stuff with when we needed to get things off our chest and needed an ear. So, what made Brooke's reaction more hurtful was that Brooke knew many things that had taken place in David and my marriage. She knew most of the issues, struggles, fights, disappointments, life-blows over the years, and she still attacked me instead of being my friend and support. On the other hand, David's closest friend, who also knew of our struggles, told David that he loved us both and would be praying for both of us. That was what I had been expecting from Brooke. Not.

I was astonished at Brooke's reaction. It hurt. I believe something snapped in her as well because she started going behind my back and trying to get David to not work with me anymore. David and I were a production team at work and decided to continue to work together. Brooke continually tried to cause problems between David and me at work. This made no sense to David or me. Brooke even told David that he did not have to pay me child support, and there was a way around it. By the way, Brooke knew I would have primary custody of Sofia and Lily and needed child support in order to keep the house. Brooke did a few other things. How do I know? Because David told me everything she was doing and saying. The situation with Brooke had gotten so bad that when David and I requested a dual meeting with our bosses to inform them of the divorce, we had to tell them what Brooke was doing so that it did not cause problems at work.

I finally had to tell Brooke that she had over-stepped her bounds, and she just needed to stay out of our business and our lives. I was not trying to mean, but she was causing constant disrupts. Yep, this was my closet friend. I cannot even begin to explain what this situation with Brooke did to me. I needed a shoulder. I needed an ally. I needed a friend. Brooke completely stabbed me in the back. Who did I have at that point to turn to for support? Keep that in mind.

To add salt to the wound and to what was already a crumbling situation, I was devastated at the reaction of David's church…the place that was our church at the time of the divorce. Remember David and I had asked that no one choose sides. We wanted everyone to show equal respect to us as we navigated through our divorce. With that being said, I was completely shattered when only one person out of the entire church even contacted me to check on me. To say that I was hurt would be an understatement. Please understand that I am not playing the victim here. I am just sharing what went on and what it did to me psychologically and emotionally in order to bring some things full circle later. Not only did I feel like the church turned its back on me, but David was also given a house-warming party by some of the church folks. Half of his new house was furnished by people that used to be friends to us both. David was even given over $3000.00 in cash and gift cards by multiple people in the church. He was given donations of household goods. People were bringing food to his house. No one even came to my house to check on me. People were calling to pray for him. My phone wasn't ringing. Some people from the congregation started avoiding me as well, and I just couldn't figure it out. I understand how a church would want to show support for its pastor, but our friends had seemingly now become his friends.

I felt alone. Very alone. Between Brooke, how the church responded, and a few other factors, I felt like I had been rejected by people who had claimed to be my friends. I had no support system. David had a huge support system. I was so hurt, and I felt like God was even playing favorites. I know that sounds ridiculous, and I also knew it was not true, but I felt completely abandoned, judged, dejected, and alone. That pit of despair was not a good place for me to be. But I now know that it was exactly where God needed me to be. God was setting me up to deal with my past once and for all. But I did not know that at the time. I had no one to talk to. I was in counseling again, but that was once a week, and I needed something tangible in my life on a daily basis. I needed someone there for me. I could not get through a day without crying. Things had gotten very argumentative between David and me at that point in time. And there was another big issue that came to a head, Arica. And the "dignity" part of our divorce went right out the window.

I do not know where you are at right now. Maybe you are in a blissful, amazing marriage. Maybe you are in a special, romantic dating situation.

Maybe you are happily, joyfully single. All I have to say to these is, "YAY!" God created us to be in a relationship with Him and with others. Any relationship has challenges. Whether it is a relationship just mentioned or a parent-child relationship. Or a friendship relationship or a thousand other possibilities. Challenges. Hurts. Regrets. Disappointments. These things can happen. And for the relationships that do not end in the way that we had hoped for, you have two decisions placed before you. You can handle the dissolving of a relationship the right way or the wrong way. And I realize there are a million different reasons why relationships come to an end. Some reasons are horrific. Some are not. But sometimes, you must rise above yourself, especially when children are involved. Sometimes the authorities have to play a part. Sometimes you can agree to disagree. With the end of the marriage between David and I, it wasn't that we weren't both hurt. We just wanted to put Sofia and Lily in a position to not be hurt as well. Of course, they were hurt and disappointed, but it could have been much worse if David and I had not worked together to make the divorce the least impactful as we could on our children. Pause. Breathe. Pray. Think. Make the right choice. Whatever that is in your situation.

Chapter 16

The Real Other Woman
The Real Testing Of My Faith

Months after the divorce, Brooke and I made up. She had tried to reconcile with me, but if anyone even mentioned her name, I just felt the knife in my back twist tighter. I am not excusing my behavior, but Brooke hurt me deeply. One day I was re-reading the scathing text she had sent me. I heard God tell me, "Delete it. You do not need a reminder of this, and it's time to get past this and let it go." So, I deleted the text. Then I felt led to call her. We set up a time for her to come to my house to talk through what had happened and try to work through it all. Brooke came over. Sofia and Lily were at home, so Brooke and I went to my bedroom to talk. I explained to Brooke how badly she had hurt me. She was my closest friend, and her text was a verbal attack on me. I explained how she turned on me when I needed her. Brooke was beyond surprised when I let her know that David had told me that she tried to talk him out of paying child support and that she was trying to cause problems between David and me at work. She had no idea I knew about all of that. Brooke tried to say that it wasn't her but her husband that had brought up the child support stuff. I replied to her that she was the person that delivered that message to David, so she was just as guilty. Brooke agreed and said that I was right and that she was sorry.

After I had said everything I needed to say and Brooke no longer tried to deny the things she had said and done behind my back, she sincerely apologized and owned up to all she had done. I then added that the main reason I called her was that God had told me that the scathing text she had sent me didn't even actually have anything to do with David and me. It was coming from her fears regarding her own marriage. That fear caused her to attack me. Brooke listened. She apologized again. I told her I forgave her and that I was willing to work on our friendship but that she would have to earn my trust again. She understood and agreed. We hugged, and our friendship started new that day. Good things happen when we listen to the leading of God. God told me to contact Brooke and get over what happened. Which was good for many reasons, one being Arica.

Arica was a divorced mother of four when she started attending our church. David and I were still married at the time. I began hearing her name from time to time, and she would call David to set up play dates with her girls and our girls. At one point, I did tell David that I thought it was inappropriate for a single woman to be calling a married man and that she should be contacting me. David just responded that Arica was shy and that they had talked at church, and she probably just felt more comfortable with him. I still didn't like it.

After the divorce, Arica did a couple more things I did not think were appropriate. I know, I divorced David, and at this point, it was none of my business. But part of it had to do with Sofia and Lily, which did make it a little bit of my business. Arica had four kids. Sofia and Lily were our kids. Arica started buying gifts for Sofia and Lily and wanted our kids and hers to spend more time together. This seemed odd to me since David said he and Arica were just friends. I felt like she was using our kids to draw closer to David.

Again, I did not have an issue with Arica and David, but I did not want Sofia and Lily used at pawns. These were just the thoughts that were developing in my head. For multiple reasons, Arica became a monumental issue between David and me. The situation eventually got ugly because I did not want her around Sofia and Lily. I felt as though there was much dishonesty going on regarding Arica. And this was when I started losing it. Seriously. I honestly believe I became a bit paranoid. Looking back now at what was going on then, I believe the divorce, although I initiated it, caused my mind to go to a place of loss, abandonment, and control. When everything around you looks to be out of control, we tend to control what we can. All the trauma of my past was about to come to an explosive head. But it needed to happen.

I had primary custody of Sofia and Lily. According to our divorce papers, David was only supposed to have the girls every other weekend and on Tuesdays until 8:00 pm. We had decided to forego the divorce papers with what my lawyer referred to as "matters of the heart." Basically, that meant that if I wanted to let David see Sofia and Lily anytime he wanted to see them, I could. David saw Sofia and Lily almost every day. I dropped them off at school, and David picked them up. They needed to see their dad, and he needed to see them. The girls could come and go between David's and my house as they wanted to. Then David started lying to me regarding Arica. David had made me some promises that he was not keeping. The sad part is that I had to find out about this situation from Sofia and Lily. Arica and I did not get along, and I wanted her influence on Sofia and Lily to be as minimal as possible. So, I rescinded and no longer let David see Sofia and Lily every day. If he could not keep his promises to me, then I would follow the divorce papers to the core.

Looking back, I now know that was not a good decision. I was not trying to hurt David. I honestly thought I was protecting our children. David was free to do whatever he wanted with whoever he wanted, but I was not going to allow Sofia and Lily to get caught up in a web of lies. Honesty is huge to me.

Arica did try to make things "right" with me, but I just would not have it. Anything to do with my kids put me in mama bear mode. If it sounds like I was starting to "lose it" a little bit, I probably was. Looking back and knowing what I know now, I think I felt threatened by another woman being in Sofia's and Lily's lives in a "motherly" role. I was hurt to see David treat this woman with so much respect and honor that I felt I did not receive during our marriage. David defended Arica in areas where he had belittled me. When I divorced David, I told him that if I did not divorce him, I was afraid that I was going to end up hating him, and I did not want to hate the father of my children. Well, I had gotten to a place where I felt like I was beginning to hate him and Arica. I had never hated anyone in my life…not even the man that raped me. And I did not like the feelings that I was having. What was more concerning is I did not know how to control the feelings I was experiencing. It scared me to be completely honest. And I wasn't liking me either. But I had no idea how to change me or what I was feeling.

My psychologist had left the practice I was going to. She had suggested other doctors at the practice, but I did not feel like starting all over with a new therapist. So, I was not in therapy for several months. But when I started feeling out of control of my own emotions, I knew I had to try one of the other doctors. Again, God's timing is always perfect. He set me up with the perfect psychologist that would help change my life.

Now I do not want you to think I was ever a danger to my kids or myself. I realistically felt fine most of the time. I had been put on anti-depressants which had helped me to quit crying all the time. I kept it together at work. I kept it together around Sofia and Lily most of the time. Although there were some spur-of-the-moment heated discussions between David and me in front of the girls that I regret. Arica was just a huge sore spot with me. And David's dishonesty was as well. David and I were on speaking terms, but where it had previously been friendly, discussions had relinquished to an as-needed basis.

I believe in the power of prayer. Never doubt that. I read my Bible daily. I read devotionals daily. I fast and pray. And trust me, I was crying out to God during this time. My emotions were all over the place. I felt like David was playing the victim. We had both agreed to keep the "why" of our divorce private, but I felt like he was playing on people's sympathies by not being honest about having done anything wrong. I had kept my end of the bargain, and when people would ask, I would still defend David's reputation and say we just had issues that drove us apart, which was the truth. I was not in a good, healthy state of mind. Not at all.

Then it happened. I was in a dead sleep one Saturday. God woke me up and told me what I needed to do. Whenever God tells me to do something, I do it. I knew exactly what I was supposed to do. I did not fight God on it. And

I knew it needed to be done. I knew Arica was flying out to Alaska that exact Saturday morning in order to pick up her youngest daughter. This daughter's dad lives in Alaska. I called David and asked if Arica had already left for the airport. He let me know that he had dropped her off at the airport early, and she was gone. So, I knew I had to do what God told me to do right then, or I would talk myself out of it. I proceeded to type out a text to Arica. I told her that I wanted to apologize to her. I went on to say that I had not been very nice to her, and that wasn't who I was. I let Arica know that I was just very hurt about so many things, and she became an easy target. I expressed how wrong of me that was. I went on to say that I had hopes that we could start over. And I ended with saying that the best thing I could wish for is that David would end up with a woman that would love our kids as her own, and I believed she would. I sent the message then let out the loudest scream I think I had ever screamed. I was glad that Sofia and Lily were at David's. I was not mad. I was not hurt. I think it was just a release of so much pain that I had allowed to build up inside of me. I fell to the ground and just screamed and cried. My pain was met with God's passion, and He just held me. God unveiled that I had directed my pain towards Arica, and when I let that go, I could breathe again. God did not want me holding onto that. It would have destroyed me.

Arica replied to the text and was very gracious. She accepted my apology and agreed we should start over. She and I get along fine now. Last summer (2020), she contacted me and expressed that she needed to talk to me. I went to her house. Arica let me know that she had been looking for a new house and found one that she loved. This house was about four doors down from my house. She was very considerate and told me there were other homes that she had toured, but she really liked the one near me. She wanted to know if it would be a problem if she bought that house. My reply was, "There will not be a problem. Buy your dream house." And she did. You can literally walk out of my back garage, through the alley, and down about three houses, and there is Arica's home. And we have never had any issues.

If at any point I have led anyone to believe that David cheated on me, he did not. I wanted to make that crystal clear.

I also stand in amazement at how God loves to show up and bring things full circle. During Spring Break of 2020 was when all hell broke out between David and me over Arica. During Spring Break of 2021, Arica showed up at my house to pick up Sofia and Lily to take them to church to help with a project. God can fix anything if you let Him.

"If you learn to trust God, you will never be disappointed."

-Michael Brown, Radio Host, Author, Apologist, Proponent of Messianic Judaism

"Delayed obedience = delayed blessing."

-Elizabeth Hasselbeck, Author, Retired Television Personality and Talk Show Host

The main reason I wanted to share the quote by Elizabeth Hasselbeck is that I shudder to think where Arica, David, and I would be right now had I not obeyed God and sent that text to Arica. Some things in life are hard. Some things in life we do not understand. But God always has our best interests at heart. And when we feel led to do something, but it doesn't "line-up" with what we think is right or fair, do it anyway. Otherwise, we are only hurting ourselves. God wants to bless us. He also wants to get our hearts healed and in the right place. But it takes us doing our part.

I have listed some songs that you may want to listen to if you have not already heard them. Music reminds my mind of the truth that is already in my heart.

"Eye of the Storm"

-By: Ryan Stevenson

"Hills and Valleys"

-By: Tauren Wells

Chapter 17

EMDR (TRAUMA) Therapy
Getting Past The Past

When my previous psychologist left the practice, and I started seeing Dr. Elena Riedo of Psychology Care Associates in Southlake, Texas, my life began to change. I first met Dr. Riedo in April of 2020. Covid was in full force, so my initial therapy sessions with Dr. Riedo were virtual in nature. I remember her asking me what all therapists seem to ask, "What do you hope to get out of therapy?" I told her that I wanted to find me again. The real me. I explained that if someone offered me a million dollars and told me that I could do whatever I wanted with it, I did not even know what I would want to do. How insane is that?

After more than forty years of abuse, judgment, losses, conforming to what other people thought I should be, and just going through a divorce, I didn't even know what I liked or who I was anymore. It required a few sessions in order to share my entire life, from my childhood to my divorce, with Dr. Riedo. She was surprised that no other therapist had ever suggested EMDR Therapy to me. My life had been riddled with trauma, and she believed that I would benefit from EMDR Therapy. Dr. Riedo presented me with a brief overview of EMDR Therapy and explained the process of such therapy. She then let me know that the EMDR sessions would need to be done in person and asked if I would be open to that. I said, without hesitation, "Yes! I just want to be healed. I just wanted to be me again." I went on to share that I did not want to bring any baggage into any new relationships in life. Dr. Riedo agreed.

EMDR Therapy is widely used to treat Trauma, PTSD, Anxiety, and Panic. EMDR is short for Eye Movement Desensitization and Reprocessing. Yes, that is a mouthful. There is countless information on the web about EMDR Therapy, but I will give you a brief overview:

"EMDR Therapy is a phased, focused approach to treating traumatic and other symptoms by reconnecting the client in a safe and measured way to the images, self-thoughts, emotions, and body sensations associated with the trauma, and allowing the natural healing powers of the brain to move towards adaptive resolution. It is based on the idea that symptoms occur when trauma and other negative or challenging experiences overwhelm the brain's natural ability to heal, and that the healing process can be facilitated and completed through bilateral stimulation while the client is re-experiencing the trauma in the context of the safe environment of the therapist's office (dual awareness)."
-Taken from: Psycom.net

"EMDR Therapy uses a three-pronged protocol: (1) the past events that have laid the groundwork for dysfunction are processed, forging new associative links with adaptive information; (2) the current circumstances that elicit distress are targeted, and internal and external triggers are desensitized; (3) imaginal templates of future events are incorporated, to assist the client in acquiring the skills needed for adaptive functioning."
–Taken from: emdr.com

Basically, you are facing your past, dealing with it, and re-programming your brain and how it reacts to trauma. You also become aware of what triggers you emotionally so you can respond appropriately. At least, that is my "plain English" version of the therapy.

During my very first EMDR Therapy session with Dr. Riedo, she discussed how the forthcoming sessions would take place and what to expect. She allowed me to ask questions, and she was very thorough with her answers. She discussed research that had been done on this type of therapy and its success rates. Dr. Riedo then picked up this large poster-board size chart of the brain that explained EMDR Therapy and how trauma affects the brain. I would not give justice to how she explained everything to me, so I am not even going to try. I will say that for my entire life, I had heard of "Fight or Flight" and how when you feel that you are in a dangerous situation, your internal gut tells you to either fight or get the heck out of the situation that you are in. What I had never heard before, though, sent me into a numb, trance-like state that left tears rolling down my face, and I could not take my eyes off the EMDR chart. There is actually a third response. There is "Fight, Flight or FREEZE." When she said "freeze," my body started tingling. I felt like I was going to pass out. Dr. Riedo could obviously see that I was overcome with emotion. She asked, "What's happening right now?" I looked at her with tears in my eyes and replied, "You just validated my entire life."

I informed Dr. Riedo that I had never heard of the third possible reaction to fearful or dangerous situations: freeze. I explained that on the night I was raped so many years ago that I did not fight back. I did not scream. I did not try to get away. I just froze and let it happen. I went on to explain that there were times over the years that I had almost even convinced myself that the rape did not happen. Then, as God would have it, many times there would be rape victims on the television show I work for, and their stories were the same as mine, and they had convinced themselves the rape didn't happen, but it did. Just because a person freezes and doesn't fight back does not make rape any less real, wrong, destructive, or life- changing. And for my entire life, whenever I felt threatened, I froze. I had built a wall around me. I had done what I needed to protect myself. I had turned inward towards self-hate. I would shut down. I did what I had done that night when I was just 17 years old. I froze, in fear, to protect me because I didn't think anyone else would ever be there to protect me. If I felt threatened, I instinctively froze or pulled back.

Instances of me doing that throughout my life flashed through my head. And that was just it. The realization of what happened, and how real it was, and how it had affected my life just brought something together at that very moment in Dr. Riedo's office. My life wasn't a total screw-up. I was not the way I was because of me. My brain had been in protection mode since I was a teenager. But it had also caused me a lot of pain along the way because I did not know what was going on in my head or how to control it. But now I did. I was ready to face my past, learn what my triggers were, and be taught how to respond and not react. I was ready for my brain to let go of the trauma and be reprogrammed to be the me that God created me to be.

The only EMDR session that I specifically want to talk about here will eventually explain many ongoing issues I have struggled with in life. It will help tie some things together. It is the session that erratically changed me. Consequently, it dealt with something that I had no clue about that was predominately negatively affecting my thoughts and actions. Dr. Riedo asked what I wanted to address at this session. I told her I wasn't really sure. So, she began the session and just started asking me questions. Suddenly in my mind, I was at the house that I lived in from the time I was born until I was 10 years old. It was as if I was watching a movie. I could see myself clearly. I was walking into our living room from the kitchen. There was no one home. I was alone. The baby me that I was seeing in this vision was about 2 years old, or so I thought. I felt very scared. Why would I be left alone? Where was everybody? Suddenly, while in Dr. Riedo's office, my right shoulder started shaking uncontrollably. It was more than a small twitch. It was causing my whole body to move. Dr. Riedo said to just let it happen because it was my body remembering the trauma and reacting to it. She asked me what I was feeling. I told her I was scared. I was alone. I was left alone. Why was I left alone? I was just a little girl.

Dr. Riedo asked, "Can you see baby Julie?" I told her, "I can." Dr. Riedo then said, "I want adult Julie to go over and pick baby Julie up." So, in my mind, I walked over to baby Julie, and I picked her up. Dr. Riedo then asked, "What is baby Julie doing?" I told her, "I am holding her. She is laughing and playing with me. She's happy. She's not alone anymore." Dr. Riedo said, "Good. Now that baby Julie is safe, I want you to do something. I want you to take baby Julie. I want you to place her in your hand. And then I want you to put her in your heart. That way, she will never be alone again." I did as Dr. Riedo instructed. The tears were running down my cheeks. My shoulder stopped trembling. I felt at total peace. This was one of the best days of my life.

For most of my life, I had felt alone. Like I had no one to go to bat for me. Like I had no one to protect me. Like I was unworthy of love. I felt alone. Now I told Dr. Riedo that I did not believe what I experienced in her office was an actual memory. She stated that although this incident might not have actually taken place, something had happened in order to make me feel that way. The result of this session was I could now rest in knowing that I was never alone and that adult me was taking care of baby me.

That may sound crazy, but it changed me. I left Dr. Riedo's office feeling a little light-headed and like I just had an out-of-body experience. That was not what happened, but I just felt different. Better. Healed in that area. I went home after that session and gathered my baby pictures. I could vividly see baby me in the vision. I knew I had a picture of the way I was visualizing me. I found it. I was only fourteen months old. I called my mom and asked if I had ever been left at the house alone by accident or anything similar, and she said no. But something had happened when I was only fourteen months old to make me feel alone and unwanted. And I felt that way for about the next 50 years of my life.

I tell you; the enemy plays dirty. Satan got in my head and caused so much pain in my life with these little thoughts: *You're alone: No one wants you. You aren't worthy of love.*

EMDR Therapy was life-changing for me. It was like a metamorphosis. I came out of a shell that I had been hiding under, that had been smothering me, for so much of my life. Between the sessions where I discovered that "freezing" during my rape and feeling alone since I was fourteen months old, I could now logically look back on my life and understand many of the bad choices I had made. EMDR also helped to explain why certain things had transpired in my life. But most of all, EMDR helped me understand my thought processes and why I had reacted to issues the way that I did… why I treated certain people the way I did. I didn't feel emotionally unstable anymore. I didn't feel out of control or the need for control.

Dr. Riedo was also able to uncover that I had severe abandonment issues as well that I previously had no clue about. I know I have mentioned abandonment issues in previous chapters, but it was not until EMDR that I was aware of the problem. Abandonment issues had caused me to be in several bad relationships because, in my mind, a bad relationship was better than being alone.

You are not your thoughts. Your behavior is caused by your thoughts. I am living proof that you can overcome your past and trauma and get your thoughts back under control. Some days are hard. If I am overly tired and something happens to hurt my feelings, and I can feel an unhealthy emotion rising up in me, I have to just stop. I have to ask myself why I am feeling that way, where the feeling is coming from, and if it is a legitimate feeling. I try to figure out the root so I can acknowledge it, think it through, then conquer it. It really is liberating to regain control of your mind. It is worth the work.

Another revelation I acquired during EMDR Therapy was that I had always thought I had "dad" issues. As mentioned in an earlier chapter, my dad wasn't around much when I was growing up to affirm me, make me feel pretty, loved, and important. On the contrary, I actually had "mom" issues, but Dr. Riedo and I were able to work through all of that.

Regardless, we were able to uncover and address so many areas of trauma in my life. I now know what triggers me and causes me to react instead of responding in certain situations. I think more clearly. I no longer feel the need to control every little thing in my life, and believe me, that is freedom in itself. I respond to hurtful situations differently. I am not paranoid. When problems arise with other people, I address the issues kindly and directly. I no longer let other people's actions control me or make me think less of me. I resolve issues based on the current situation. I no longer let the past control the present. I have peace. I can breathe. And the walls around me have continued to crumble down. I feel like I am me. I feel like I know me. I know who I was meant to be, created to be. I felt the weight of the world lifted off me during my EMDR sessions and continuing therapy. I felt guilt lifted off me. I felt shame lifted off me. I felt life breathed into me. Where shame had told me I was something wrong, I now know that was not true at all. I felt free.

So much healing came out of my sessions with Dr. Riedo. And I continue to see her. Life isn't perfect. We go through stuff. Dr. Riedo continues to help me to know how to deal with stuff that life throws at me. I now have the knowledge to navigate life and my emotions in a positive, healthy way. But the unveiling of my traumatic past and how it caused me to act or react in certain ways was not over. Wait until you hear what Dr. Riedo uncovered and taught me how to deal with in an upcoming chapter.

God is good. Bottom line. I am a Christian, and I believe in the power of prayer. I am also smart enough to know that God has given us the ability to know when we need to seek outside help. The mind is delicate yet complicated. And I believe there are some journeys that you cannot make alone. Finding an amazing, compassionate, trained psychologist who has the knowledge to balance the scientific side of life and understands the spiritual side of life as well is what saved me from continuing to spiral downward. I had reached my breaking point. I gave God all the shattered pieces of my life, and He directed me to specific people that could help put me back together. Nothing is too big for God. But it all begins with admitting you have a problem and doing your part to get the healing that you need.

Chapter 18

Fear Factor And Control Issues
Peace Over Frenzy

When a person experiences traumatic events in one's life, there are multiple possible outcomes or reactions, obviously. For me, the fact that I had been judged, mistreated, and even raped during my teen years resulted in the development of massive fear and control issues. I certainly did not realize I had these issues back then, but I do now. How I was regarded or treated by some of the people in my small town due to my brothers' actions was just the beginning of my fear of people and what people thought of me. Bottom line, the treatment I endured was emotional abuse inflicted on me. Fear would have a continual grip on me for years to come.

Sadly, fear will cause you to make wrong decisions, time and time again. Fear will cause you to freeze. Fear will cause you to lose your true identity. Fear can cause you to withdraw from life. In order to protect yourself, you might build walls, but those walls also keep people from loving you and getting close to you. Fear can destroy you. Remember, your emotions will lie to you. There is a reason that the phrase "Do not fear" is written 365 times in the Bible. God knew the powerful, destructive impact of fear. He wanted to remind us, every single 365 days, that fear is a liar. But, alas, we are human. We are frail. We make mistakes. But we do have the power within us to overcome fear. And I am not talking about things such as the fear of flying or fear of spiders and so forth. I am referring to deep, emotional, paralyzing fear that keeps you from living a full life.

Then there is "control." I deeply felt as though I lost control of my life when I was 17 when the rape took place. My hope was to stay pure and save myself for marriage. That was my decision. That was what I wanted and desired. But that was taken away from me. I felt I had lost all control of my life. And what was the resulting factor of this? It turned me into a control freak. I could not control or take back the fact that I had been raped. As a result, I was going to control every single, little, minuscule, "wee" thing that I could.

Now mind you, I did not find this out about me until much later in life. If someone had told me back then that I had become a control freak, the thought would have been inconceivable to me. Really? Unfortunately, yes. If you are a control freak but you are not unaware of this nasty pitfall, one way to realize it is if you notice that you make the people around you nuts at times. You are trying to be perfect, and you are trying to conform those around you into perfection as well. Guess what? It is not going to work for you, and you are affecting the natural state of other individuals' lives.

Stop making people crazy! Stop pushing people away due to your control issues. What does this look like? For me, I became a neat freak. Now that is not a bad thing in some situations. But, if you are killing yourself to always keep a spotless house in case someone stops by, you are, in fact, losing valuable time with your family. And whoever stops by probably would not care if you have dirty dishes in the sink anyway. This may not seem like a big thing, but it was. If the girls left their shoes in the middle of the floor, I would move the shoes by the front door. If the girls left toys out, I immediately returned the things to their rooms. If the girls had friends spending the night, I would clean the entire house because I did not want anyone thinking I was a lazy slob that had an unkempt house. That's not healthy. So, let your kids be kids. Let them make messes. Let them do experiments. Although I did have to tell Lily several times not to put glue down the sink as she was making "slim." Enjoy every minute you can with your kids. You only have them for a number of years before they are gone and living their own lives.

What could I control? Well, quite frankly, a great number of things. And I slowly slipped into what I now call "Perfectionism at its worse." Yes, I became a perfectionist. Doing your best is a good thing. For instance, getting good grades or being disciplined in living a healthy lifestyle. But I could be over the top. I remember telling David before we got married, "If you allow me to control you, I will. And I won't even know I'm doing it, so you will have to kindly let me know." David knew about my past. I had been single until I was thirty, so I only had me to rely on for so many years. During those single years, I became a pro at controlling my surroundings. I left it up to David to tell me if I was being controlling. Yeh, what husband is going to step into that mud? Actually, David did a good job, and he did help me to "chill out" as time went by.

I remember when I moved away from my small hometown. One big thought in my head was, "I am going to make something out of my life and show them (my townspeople) that I AM somebody." Yes, that is how messed up my mind was. The truth was I had nothing to prove to anyone. God is an audience of One, and He is the only One I need to please. He loves me completely. Regrettably, I did not realize that precious, simple bit of knowledge back then. I was too hurt. I was too blinded by my emotions. Consequently, I went into my chosen career field for all the wrong reasons. In my thought process, I was thinking a Broadcast Journalism degree would be perfect. I was going to be on television. I was going to prove that I was "worthy." I was going to "be somebody." That sounds so ridiculous now. It even makes me laugh a bit because while at Belmont University when we had to do on-screen assignments, I was scared to death. Maybe that is normal, but I decided working behind the camera instead of in front of it would be a better path for me. In hindsight, I now know those overwhelming feelings were just a part of my low self-worth talking. In truth, I did not feel good enough. Who would want to see me report the news or host a television show? Thankfully, as always,

God is in the business of turning things around. Working in television has been a huge blessing to me for a multitude of reasons.

I believe my perfectionism and control issues became evident to me more so when I had Sofia. I was killing myself trying to be the perfect mom with the perfect child that was always dressed cute and never stunk. The perfect mom that had all toys put away in their proper place, no spit up on the floor, and no stinky diapers in the garage in case someone did indeed stop by. The perfect mom keeping healthy, doing whatever school fund-raising event that was going on while holding down and performing at top speed as a Television Producer for an international Christian talk show. The perfect mom that did not look disheveled and showed up for all the church events. The perfect mom that still made it to baby and wedding showers, so no one thought I slighted them. The perfect mom that supported her pastor husband. The perfect mom that… someone slap me out of this, please! No one did. But who would?

There is no way of knowing, but I do believe I was suffering from postpartum depression for an entire year after Sofia was born. I knew nothing about it. David knew nothing about it. But we were in survival mode dealing with my nasty infection from the C-section and having a newborn with serious medical issues. Plus, my mother-in-law questioned every single thing David and I did as parents. I was existing yet not existing. I was going through the motions. Approximately one year after Sofia was born, David and I were in church service, and I went down to the altar for prayer, and something broke off of me. I was crying, and I told David I just felt different. The depression I had felt for an entire year after Sofia was born was gone. David's exact words were, "I feel like I have my wife back."

I have no idea precisely when perfectionism started breaking off of me. I admit that I still deal with aspects of perfectionism, but I no longer let it affect the people around me like it did. I now know when it is raising its ugly little head, and I "nip it in the bud!" In fact, you would probably laugh if you came to my house for a visit. The master bedroom is downstairs, so I consider downstairs at least partially "my domain," so it is usually clean. Usually… not always. Take a few steps to the second floor and… disaster area. Sofia and Lily like the "lived-in" look, and I have come to be okay with that. Live and learn. I am a work in progress and getting a little better every single day. With that being said, if you stop by my house and there are kid's uniforms, basketballs, footballs, shoes, and backpacks on my floor, dirty dishes in the sink, and I haven't swept the floor in days, I don't want to hear it. (laughter) Just move the stuff over, have a seat, and let's spend some time together. And if the house stinks like a school locker room, I will spray something I bought at Bath and Body Works. Having kids has taught me just how short life is, and I would rather spend time with them than hours cleaning my less-than-perfect household every day. Can I get an amen? Take time to forgive yourself for not being perfect. It really is a cleansing and freeing experience to just be you.

And as I mentioned in a previous chapter, when I got over my fear of being alone, because I am never alone, so much of my life changed. I had no idea that "aloneness" was even such an issue in my life and what a strangling effect it had on me. But now that I know the root of my issues and what triggers me and why, I know how to realize what is going on and respond appropriately instead of reacting in an unwise and unhealthy way. YES! I believe that God loves to make us face what we fear so we, in turn, grow into the people that He created us to be. I have discussed fear, control, depression, and perfectionism in this chapter. I would like to end this chapter with some quotes that I have kept in a notebook.

"Those who cannot remember the past are condemned to repeat it."

--George Santayana, Philosopher

"The peace you seek is on the other side of the war within."
"The world within you will create the world around you."

--Erwin McManus, from "The Way of the Warrior"

"Courage doesn't mean we are never scared. Courage is being afraid and taking action anyway, despite our fear."

--Ruth Soukup, Author, Entrepreneur, Product Creator

"You gain strength, courage, and confidence by every experience in which you really stop to look fear in the face. You are able to say to yourself, 'I have lived through this horror. I can take the next thing that comes along.' You must do the thing you think you cannot do."

--Eleanor Roosevelt, Former First Lady

I also want to mention some songs that, if you have not heard them, I believe could move your spirit, change your perspective, and help you find peace. Hop online and take a listen. I love these:

"No Longer Slaves"

-By: Bethel Music with Jonathan David and Melissa Helser

"Peace Be Still"

-By: Hope Darst

"God Turn It Around"

-By: Church In The City

"Just Be Held"

-By: Casting Crowns

"The Breakup Song"

-By: Francesca Battistelli

Chapter 19

Dating Again
The New Digital Age Of Dating Apps

I actually just giggled a little after typing the chapter title. The thought of dating again was not on my radar. I would like to point out that I feel very blessed that I have friends in my life of all ages. I have people I talk to that are in their 20s all the way up through people in their 70s. I feel that we can learn from all the generations. But then came the day that I wanted to skip over the younger generation. I am kidding. Let me explain.

About nine months after my divorce, I was at work and taking a break from editing on one lovely afternoon. The young gal who worked at our front desk, Jenna, and I were discussing some guys she had been talking to online. This conversation brought up the whole subject of dating apps. Jenna is young enough to be my daughter. Jenna asked me, "So, you gonna get on any dating apps?" I looked at her like she was insane. She just cut me a look and said, "You know, you haven't dated in twenty years, and apps are the way people meet these days." I just kind of giggled and decided to let that conversation go.

At the same time, I must admit, I am a hopeless romantic, and I knew I wanted to find love and have someone to share life with. I knew a lady at church that had met her husband through a dating app, and they were several years older than me. I had a friend from Nashville that met her fiancé on a dating website. Her advice to me was, and this was her talking, not me, "You'll have to work your way through a lot of frogs but if you hang in there, your Prince Charming is out there." That was not the vote of confidence that I needed for online dating.

It was 2020, and Covid was in full force. Due to this inconvenient factor, there were only two places I ventured out to, which were work and church. Work was out of the question, and church, well, if you met someone at church, then things just didn't work out, one of you would have to find a new church. It's okay to laugh. I did. So, I prayed about my current, single situation and decided to move forward and try some dating websites. This was completely new territory to me. You could have just as easily asked me to pilot a spaceship to the moon. I wasn't the best at technology, but I was able to figure everything out. I set up my profile which consisted of answering some questions, writing a description of myself and what I was "looking for in a man," and adding some pictures. I uploaded my profile and almost threw up. What had I just gotten myself into? Was this really the way I wanted to meet men? No. But, as Jenna told me, this was the way of the future. Now the "wait and see" began.

The waiting on two of the websites was not long. Almost immediately, it was obvious that I was going to "just say no" to those particular websites. The other one that I decided to stick with was interesting, to say the least. Welcome to the new world of how to meet potential dates, ugh. It was fun and exciting and scary and intimidating all at the same time. What I wrote in my profile was very specific and honest. I did not want to be random about what I was looking for in someone. I stressed that I was a Christian and wanted a like-minded individual. You would be amazed, disgusted, and probably laugh, and even think "what?" to many of the messages I received. Some were quite suggestive in nature. Moving on.

All in all, online dating was not the best experience for multiple rea-sons. I do not want to discourage anyone from going on dating websites because I do know people that have found lasting relationships in this man-ner. But seriously, I could share some stories with you that would turn your stomach or make you roll your eyes. My time with dating websites was not all bad, however. I feel that if you learn a lesson from something, especially a lesson that makes you a better person, then it is a good thing. I did meet two men on a very popular dating website that I did go on dates with. I would like to share a little bit about what I learned from each of these men because they both added something to my life. God always has a plan.

Chapter 20

Julian: Dating After Divorce
Learning To Feel Again

Yes, that was his real name. The only reason I am not changing his name is that there are plenty of men named Julian in Texas, so his identity is not at risk. We were Julian and Julie. I thought it was cute. Believe it or not, my parents' names are Clyde and Clydean. True fact. When I met David's parents, after I told Tom that my parents' names were Clyde and Clydean, he told me I could just call him and Joyce Tom and Tomette. Always a jokester.

At this point in time, I had been divorced for about nine months. I felt as though I had achieved a lot of personal and emotional healing and was ready to date again. I was still in therapy with Dr. Riedo and kept her informed about all of my dating decisions. I was nervous and excited all at the same time. Reading through so many online profiles of men was giddy and gut-wrenching. Why? The obvious reason is due to the fact I had not dated in twenty years. I was recently divorced. And I felt like looking at these online profiles was like, well, when I was a child, and the JCPenney Christmas catalog came in the mail, and I pointed to my dad and mom what I wanted. This was just new and strange to me, reading profiles to see what man I might want to start a conversation with. I most definitely prayed about anyone I might talk to. There are scammers out there, and you must be careful. Julian and I started chatting on the dating website daily, and after about a week, we exchanged phone numbers and texted multiple times for another week.

I have no problem admitting I was very attracted to him. Julian and I had many things in common. I truly enjoyed our conversations.

Julian lived about an hour away from me, but one day he let me know that he was taking his child to his brother's house. Julian mentioned that his brother did not live too far from me. With this, Julian wanted to know if it was too soon for us to meet. I told him that I was looking forward to meeting him. It was of utmost importance to me that on my profile on this dating website, I was very direct that I am a Christian and that I am very active in my faith. I was not looking for a fling. I also stated that I was looking for someone emotionally stable. I let it be known that even though I was past 50, I still had kids at home. I wanted to meet someone and become friends and see where it might lead. Again, I said I was a Christian and very active in my faith, went to church every week, and worked for a ministry. Julian professed to be a Christian, and I believe he loved the Lord. I am not judging him, but he was very forward and let me know that he is a very "sensual" person and what he "expected" early on in the relationship if we started dating. My reply to him was, "That's not happening." He told me, "We'll see." Trust me, I know I should have stopped speaking to him at that exact moment.

There were all kinds of red flags when I had started dating David that I ignored. If David had been looking, he would have seen some as well on my part. It should have been an immediate red flag when Julian made sexual comments, but I actually liked him and wanted to see if this was really who he was or not. Julian seemed like a great dad, a good guy, just a bit "cocky." I was not very wise, and we did meet. He came to my house, and we talked for about five hours before he had to leave to get his child. Julian and I talked about any and everything we could think of. Our meeting turned out to be a pleasant experience.

Julian and I continued to chat daily. But it was odd at times. I literally felt like I was dealing with two different people. My friend Brooke insisted she thought Julian was married and playing me. One day Julian would be sweet and romantic. Other days he would be very suggestive and aggressive.

And there were times he was flat-out mean. One day he accused me of being selfish and narcissistic and said I was "gaslighting" him. I did not even know what that meant and had to look it up. The subject of sex kept coming up and became a subject of contention between us for multiple reasons. Mainly because it wasn't happening. Yes, I know, I should have just blown him off, but when he was nice, he was really nice. Keep in mind that I had a long history of drawing men to me that were absolutely not good for me. I think it's the "woman" in me. We want to fix things, fix people. But that's not our job, and we are not even qualified for it. I am positive that only God can intervene and do such things. Uh, my bad.

Dr. Riedo asked me about Julian during every session since she knew I had started dating again. She thought it was a very toxic relationship between Julian and me. She was right, but I wasn't ready to throw in the towel. I will explain why soon. Text conversations between Julian and I were getting a little out of control. I tried to end things with Julian twice but then kept responding to his texts. We each felt like the other was sending mixed messages. We both probably were. Brooke and another friend were telling me to run. Run like crazy. One should heed the advice of good friends. I know that now. But here is what they did not get; prior to Julian getting a bit out of hand, he did something for me that he didn't even know he was doing. To be very honest and specific, Julian taught me to "feel" again. The best way I know how to explain what I am trying to communicate is that I had been unhappy in my marriage for so many years. With all the things that David and I had gone through and our own individual issues, the majority of feelings I had felt for the past years were hurt, loneliness, anger, and eventually bitterness. That's just where I was in life after all the things David and I had experienced. But with Julian, I went from numb to another level. Despite the craziness, he helped me to feel again. I felt pretty. I felt desired. I felt like someone was interested in me just for me. I felt. I just felt good feelings. And Julian brought those feelings out. And they needed to come out. I needed to "feel" good emotions again.

But that was also a little dangerous when I was still walking through some healing processes and learning to recognize triggers and overcome them. See, Julian was filling a void in my life, but he was also trying to control me. And he was messing with my mind. In the end, we got into a huge argument… via text. Yes… ugh. It got ugly, and, yes, it was over. And it needed to be over. But in the end, I do not regret my brief time with Julian. Why? There are multiple reasons. One, I already mentioned, he helped me feel something other than hurt, and that truly did open up a part of my heart that had just been closed for so long where men are concerned. And when it was over, I asked God, "Why? Why would you let this person in my life just to have it end this way? I asked You to protect me from any man I didn't need to speak to before I joined that website, so, why?" God answered me and said, "You're asking the wrong question. You should be asking for what purpose did I allow this in your life." It was like a lightbulb turning on, and I instantly knew what God meant. I came to realize that Julian helped me to feel again. It may sound nuts, but when you have been broken, and you just become numb in so many ways, it is like a breath of fresh air to feel feelings that had been dormant for a long time. So, it was a good experience. God just had to get me to see things from another perspective.

Not only that, Dr. Riedo was able to clarify and teach me certain things in regards to my time with Julian. She made no bones about it and let me know it was a toxic relationship. Dr. Riedo asked me to make her a promise. She directly expressed that texting should only be used for short messages like, "I'm running late," or "Can you pick up some bread at the store," or "I'm thinking of you!" Texting is NOT for deep, possibly controversial conversations. The good doctor told me that I would be amazed at how many men and women she had counseled who had relationship issues over misinterpreted texts. Yeh! I get that now.

Dr. Riedo, at one point in therapy, asked me if I knew how many times I referred to myself as "stupid" or mentioned that I made a "stupid" decision? I had no idea I referred to myself as stupid. Dr. Riedo told me the number of times I had said it just in a few moments of talking to her. I was surprised. I later asked Brooke, "In our conversations, do I ever refer to myself as stupid?" Her reply was, "Yeh, all the time!" Dr. Riedo made me promise that I would no longer refer to myself as stupid. Why is this important? Well, let me explain it to you. First of all, I believe the root of me referring to myself as stupid goes all the way back to me getting pregnant the second time. Remember, I said, "Stupid! Stupid! Stupid Me!" My subconscious remembered that incident… that one moment in time. But due to it, from that point on in my life, I just thought I was stupid. And that was how I referred to myself. This is about to tie a lot of stuff together, so bear with me.

Dr. Riedo asked me to focus on the feelings of "being stupid" and, whenever those feelings come up, try and figure out where they are coming from. She explained the reason this is so important is that the word "stupid" brings "shame." Consequently, when we walk in shame, we attract bad things and bad people into our lives because we think we don't deserve any better. Remember, shame tells you that you ARE something "wrong." I had felt wrong and stupid for the better part of my adult life. Dr. Riedo told me to imagine it as an "aura." Your aura is viewed as a "vibe" or atmosphere that is emanating from your being that you are projecting to the world. Dr. Riedo told me that when you walk around in shame, you attract bad things. Your aura attracts the very things and people you do not need in your life. You are not open to the "good" in life. Shame is not open to love because you don't think you deserve it.

Now, this was all going on subconsciously with me. For years. I had no idea. Dr. Riedo went on to say that this ongoing self-description of myself would explain why I dated mostly "not so good guys" during my life. The aura that was surrounding me attracted the very men I didn't need in my life. Now, I did date a couple of good guys, but not many. Everything was coming together and making sense to me now. I regretted the fact that I was in my 50s before I discovered all of this but better late than never. Please, please, please, if you have gone through traumatic experiences, get help. There is so much life to be lived on the other side of guilt, shame, regret, loss, and pain. And you deserve so much more.

You must love, respect, and honor yourself for the incredible person that God crafted you to be. The enemy got into my mind at such a young age that I was blinded to so many things, and I made such bad decisions. I did not love me, and I attracted men that did not truly love me either. I decided it was time to shake my aura up! I was learning to love me, and I wanted a good man that would love me just for me. Just as I am. That sounds like heaven.

A few more things that I learned from Dr. Riedo should be mentioned before I move on. She told me not to place so many expectations or demands on other people due to my control issues or in response to my abandonment issues. If that does not make total sense, I will give some examples. One example would be if people do not text you back in the amount of time that you thought they should have, don't freak out and blow them off. They might just be busy. That would be a feeling of insecurity stemming from abandonment issues. Other examples would be to stop assuming, quit thinking the worse, allow time for things to develop naturally. I will say that Dr. Riedo has worked in these areas with me diligently, and I have come a long way in those two areas. Alas, but I am still a work in progress. At least now I recognize when the issues come up and can deal with them accordingly and appropriately. My previous fear of being alone would tell me that it was better to be with a not-so-good guy instead of being alone. Wrong! I have completely cleared that hurdle and will no longer accept less than God's best for me. I am never alone, and I would rather be single than with someone who does not honor, respect, and love me. You should expect the same whether you are a man or woman. Live like you are expecting the best because that is exactly what you deserve. Don't settle!

I had a hard time loving myself or even liking myself. If you ever feel that way, then just remember that loving yourself is not selfish. In fact, it's a command:

"Love the Lord your God with all your heart and with all your soul and with all your mind and with all your strength. The second is this: Love your neighbor as yourself. There is no commandment greater than these."

-Mark 12:30-31 (NIV)

One more disclosure before I conclude this chapter. If you feel like your aura needs a little adjustment, it all starts with you. For me, personally, there is a song that gives my aura a little ripple when it needs it. You can ask Sofia and Lily, if we are in the car or at home, if this song comes on, I'm going to dance. Please feel free to listen and bust a move. Just sayin…

"Shake"

-By: MercyMe

Let's throw this one in here too…

"High Hopes"

-By: Panic At The Disco

Chapter 21

_____

Freddy: Dating Round Two
The Best Is Yet To Come

After the brief, problematic courtship with Julian, I decided to shut down my profile on the dating website I had joined. Regardless, I continued to receive emails with "possible matches." I did not know it then, but the website will continue to send you profiles of men in hopes that you will rejoin the dating game. After a bit of pondering, I concluded that I had already paid for membership on the website, so I decided to go back on and re-open my profile. One message I had received was from a man that lived in another state, so I saw no point in replying to his message. I honestly did not see the point of long-distance dating. This man was attractive. Even so, you really do need to put much consideration into who you respond to on these websites. One day this man messaged me again and asked what he had to do to get me to respond to him. I then decided to check out his profile. His profile mentioned that he was a Christian, but so did some of these other men's profiles that had asked me some obscene questions. My conclusion was that this man seemed really nice. So I decided to reply to him. I immediately asked him about his faith. Some individuals may think that is too direct and too personal to ask right up front, but Dr. Riedo taught me something else that I intended to implement when dating.

Dr. Riedo firmly suggested that I needed to make a list of "non-nego-tiables." She explained that men and women alike jump into relationships for reasons based solely on attraction or wealth or sex or common interests. But when these people go deeper into the relationship, there are not enough tangible bonds to hold it together. That is not exactly how Dr. Riedo worded it, but that is how I interpreted what she was expressing to me. She recommended that I make a distinct list of non-negotiables in reference to dating. Dr. Riedo also proposed that I write down specific characteristics any potential date must exhibit before I even consider going on a date with him. Without any thought, the top of the list for me is that he needs to be a Christian. That is a non-negotiable. There were other qualities on the list as well, such as he would have to be a non-smoker, not into the "party" lifestyle, must love kids, and, well, the list had several characteristics listed. Therefore, with the variety of the other tools taught to me by Dr. Riedo, I had no problem asking this man, Freddy, about his faith.

Freddy had no issue with opening up about his faith. He had been a Christian most of his life. He had participated in missionary work. Freddy had raised his family in a Christian home. He attended church and was active in his faith. At that point, the conversations continued.

Freddy and I hit it off immediately. We were both aware of the hours between us, seeing that he lived in another state. This should have been a red flag, but we truly enjoyed talking to each other and had an enormous amount of similar interests. Freddy and I began communication via the dating website. As time went on, Freddy and I exchanged phone numbers. We texted or spoke on the phone daily. We talked about our childhoods, our families and growing up, places we had traveled, our kids, foods we liked, our jobs, our hobbies, our churches, our bucket lists, and the list goes on and on. The day came when Freddy asked if we could meet. I had no problem saying yes. Seeing that it was going to be a bit of a drive for him, Freddy asked if he could come in the morning, and we could spend the entire day together. He suggested that we could meet, chat, go somewhere fun, and afterward, he wanted to cook dinner for me. I was all in. I was beyond excited about meeting Freddy.

BEST FIRST DATE EVER!!! Let me just say that Freddy completely blew me away. I could have never imagined how amazing this date would be. Freddy arrived at my house on a Saturday morning. I went out to meet him and give him a hug. I am a hugger! If you and I ever meet, be prepared. I hug people I just met. I don't care. Ask my kids; I am a hugger. What made this date so amazing and perfect is that as Freddy was unloading his truck, it was obvious that he had really been listening to me during our conversations. That may sound like that word I am not supposed to say (stupid), but I don't think a lot of people actually listen at times. I don't say that to be disrespectful in any way, but conversations can be lacking these days. I digress. Again, it was obvious that Freddy had listened to every single thing we had talked about before we met. He presented me with flowers, roses. I love flowers in general, but roses are my favorite. Freddy had gone shopping at Hobby Lobby and bought a rustic vase to put the flowers in. Black is one of my favorite colors, and he had bought these black feather-like stems and mixed them in with the roses. The arrangement of flowers and feathers was beautiful. He had bought a cute and silly gift for Lily. Freddy began to unpack multiple baking utensils he had purchased as well as melting chocolate so we could make chocolate-covered strawberries for dessert. He started unloading the ice chest from his truck that contained salmon, steak, and shrimp along with brussel sprout salad that he was going to prepare for dinner. Freddy knew that I am fond of "The Tree of Life," so he shopped and found an art kit that would allow me to make a "Tree of Life" to hang on my wall. He gave me a card but told me I could read it later after he left. This sweet man even brought movies for us to watch after dinner. I was impressed.

Once Freddy had finished bringing in all the things he had brought, we headed out for historic downtown Grapevine, Texas. If you ever come to the Dallas-Fort Worth areas of Texas, you should make the quick trip to Grapevine. And yes, Freddy was a perfect gentleman and opened his truck door and every other door we walked into throughout the day. It had been a long time since I had had someone do that for me. It certainly is those little gestures that I notice and remember.

The weather was beautiful, and historic downtown Grapevine is a wonderful place to hang out and get to know someone. There are all kinds of quaint little shops to browse through. You also have your pick of wonderful places to eat. There is an amazing farmer's market, an old train station that still operates, a movie theater, wineries, and snack shops. Freddy and I went through several stores. He was so considerate and even bought small gifts for Sofia and Lily. We stopped for a light lunch and shared an omelet and salad. The conversation between us was non-stop. We really were amazed at how much we had in common. After lunch, Freddy and I walked around town more before heading back to my house. Once at my place, we decided to make the chocolate-covered strawberries. My microwave was broken, so we tried the double-broiler method, but it just was not melting the chocolate properly. We pressed forward with determination and laughter. In the end, we completed dessert and put the strawberries in the refrigerator. They were not the prettiest chocolate-covered strawberries, but we had an amusing and fun time making them. And the taste? Not bad at all, if I must say.

It was too early for dinner, so Freddy and I decided to watch one of the movies he had brought. We sat on the couch and held hands, and Freddy was a perfect gentleman. After the movie, he cooked me a delicious meal of steak, shrimp, and salmon with brussel sprout salad. It was delicious. I was impressed. To top it off, Freddy insisted on washing all the dishes and putting them away. Bonus points! After dinner and conversation, we went back to the couch to watch the second movie. Throughout the movie, Freddy was kissing my hand, which I found to be very sweet. Again, he was a perfect gentleman. Freddy hung out at my house until about 10:30 pm. He then had the long four-hour drive home. Once his truck drove out of sight, I read the card he had bought me. I know people might think this was way too soon, but he let me know that he had started falling for me before we even met in person. He really touched my heart.

I did not feel obsessive with Freddy. I did not feel scared. I did not feel controlling. I felt perfect peace. Why? Because he proved to me that he had been really listening in our conversations, he went out of his way to make our first date special, and he was a gentleman. I was not accustomed to all of that, and it was all quite delightful and sweet. Freddy and I continued to talk and text non-stop. Two weeks after our first date, we decided we would each drive half-way and meet up in a town just across the Texas border and spend the day together. Four hours was a hefty drive for a date, so I did not mind driving to meet him half-way. Freddy and I talked, drove around, walked by a lake, ate, and talked some more. But it was more than that; we dreamed together, and it was beautiful.

Freddy told me he loved me even before our second date. I guess that did not seem too strange to me because David had told me he loved me on our first date. When two people take the time to get to know each other, feelings can happen quickly. The only reason I even share this is in order to explain something very important. Just as Julian had taught me to "feel" again, Freddy demonstrated to me what the true concept of love between a man and a woman was. And it had nothing to do with sex because that was not happening in our relationship. Think about it. Almost every man in my life, throughout my life, that claimed to love or care about me hurt me. My father was pretty much absent in my life for a time. A boyfriend raped me. Another boyfriend had shared needles during his drug use and thought he might have given me HIV. Oh, and he cheated on me as well. One other boyfriend beat me up and held me hostage at gunpoint. I could go on, but I hope you get what I am trying to express. I was important to Freddy. He was protective of me. He was caring and respectful towards me. He listened to what I had to say. He made me feel special. He was romantic instead of pushy. He saw me.

But the four-hour distance between us was beginning to wear a bit. Freddy still has children at home. I still have children at home. Neither of us could move to be closer to the other, and we had to start addressing these issues. Long-distance relationships can and do work, but they can be challenging. My thought to Freddy was that I was going to just live in the moment and see where the road might take us. He agreed to try and do so as well. Freddy would send me the sweetest YouTube music videos of love songs and tell me he was thinking of me daily. I was experiencing feelings that I had not had in years. And it scared me a little, but I loved it. What Freddy and I had was peaceful and sweet and good. But knowing Freddy loved me and the fact that we had started talking about a future together brought up something that I had to face. If we were seriously considering a future together, and we were, I had to face my biggest fear and tell Freddy the truth. The truth that I had found out several years prior when petitioning for the adoption of Lily. The truth that I had contracted Herpes.

I was not sure if, legally, a person is required to share that information. Freddy and I were not sexually active, but I had to tell him. To say I was scared would have been an understatement. I was terrified. I had never breathed a word of this diagnosis to anyone other than doctors. There was no point. Why would I share this information with people? Herpes is harmless. The virus is not contagious in any way other than sexual contact, so there was no reason for anyone to know this about me. But if you are discussing a future, marriage with someone, sex will eventually come into the relationship. Freddy needed to know so that he could make the decision on whether he wanted to continue in a relationship with me. I had to tell him and tell him immediately. But how?

I will be the first to admit that I went about telling Freddy in an entirely immature way. I will not even try to back out of that fact. But I had never had to face this kind of situation before. And I truly did not know what to do. Therefore, I resorted to what I know. I write. So, I decided to write Freddy a letter. Please no eye-rolls. It was one of the hardest things that I ever had to do, but it had to be done. In this brief letter, I explained how I came to find out that I had Herpes. I went on to explain that the virus is not life-threatening and is basically harmless, but there are potential issues. I explained that I had no symptoms but that I was on medication to "just be safe." I told him to feel free to read up on the virus. Then I ended the letter by saying that if this information was too much for him and he no longer wanted to date me, I completely understood. Signed, sealed, waiting to be delivered.

On our third date, I cooked an amazing, if I must say so myself, Tex-Mex meal completely from scratch. Freddy and I spent the afternoon watching the Texas versus OU game. Nothing like an afternoon of football and Mexican food. After the game, Freddy and I went shopping for haybales and Fall decorations for my front yard. I am totally into the holidays. I love Fall and all that is a part of the Fall season. The changing colors of the tree leaves, busting out the Fall and Winter wardrobe, decorating the house, candles that smell of cinnamon, and just everything. Freddy had bought some flowers for my flowerbed, and when we returned to my house, he planted them. So sweet. We made the decision to go out for dinner. There is not a lack of restaurants in the Dallas-Fort Worth Metroplex. Once dinner and conversation wrapped up, we went back to my house to watch a movie. When it came time for Freddy to leave, I hugged him, gave him the letter, and kissed him goodbye. Freddy and I often gave objects of affection to one another in person or by mail, so he just took the letter and headed out the door. As I closed the door behind Freddy, I sunk to the floor and just started to cry. Why? Because I felt like this could have been the last time I would ever see him. I cried for a long time. Sadness filled my heart. But I did the right thing by telling him the truth.

Well, Freddy dumped me. The next morning, I had multiple texts on my phone. Freddy had driven about half-way home the previous night then pulled over to take a nap. Prior to napping, he decided it would be a good time to read my letter. Of course, it was not what he expected. Several texts and phone calls were exchanged between us. At first, Freddy was scared. He had gone online and read some stuff about Herpes that is not true. You cannot get Herpes from kissing. HSV-1, which is basically cold sores, is a form of Herpes. And yes, HSV-1 can be transmitted by kissing. HSV-2 can only be transmitted by sexual contact. Sex was not taking place between Freddy and me. I assured him he was safe and could not have contracted the virus from me by kissing. Freddy was a little upset that I had not told him about the Herpes sooner. My explanation to Freddy was that I personally did not think it was something to be discussed on a first date. I furthermore stated that there would be no point in discussing it at all unless a relationship was to take a turn towards being serious. That is just my personal thought on the subject. Freddy and I had only been on two dates. I then told him about the Herpes situation on the third date. Freddy obviously had several questions that I had the knowledge for and was able to answer for him. We had discussions about Herpes for several days. We reached the point in our dialogue that I ultimately told him that if he did not trust and believe me, then subsequently, he should go and get tested. In the end, Freddy told me that the thought of possibly contracting Herpes was just too much for him. Our future and our dreams were over. Undeniably I was hurt. I was crushed. My heart was broken. I cried for weeks, but I understood. I was not mad at Freddy. Not at all. Just hurt. I hurt more with this dating relationship because I genuinely cared for Freddy. But again. I understood. Who knows, I might have done the same thing in this situation if the roles were reversed.

Freddy would continue to text me off and on, which was confusing to me. He wanted to remain friends. I told him that would not be possible. "Just friends" would be too difficult and complicated for me. I missed him, but if we were no longer going to be dating, then I needed closure so I could move forward. Closure did not mean that the situation hurt any less. I cried. I cried a lot. But in God's goodness, some amazing things happened in the following weeks that I would love to share with you.

I had been praying and fasting because I was completely beside myself. I was sad. I was numb. I was experiencing deep pain because of what I had shared and was rejected for. One day I went home during my lunch break. I was praying, and I felt like God told me two things, "Quit assuming and quit trying to figure things out!" I admit that I am very analytical at times, but I knew what God was saying. However, I was not quite ready to hear it. Everything was still so fresh. God wanted me to just release the hurt to Him and trust Him. God did not want me overthinking this issue with Freddy and dwelling on it all. What had happened, happened. And as unpleasant as it was, God was still in control. I knew all of this, but I just felt broken inside. Again. I had hoped and believed that things would turn out better this time. It is at times like these, those moments of uncertainty, that all we can do is just trust and wait on God. And the waiting is typically not easy. At least not in my experiences.

When you trust and wait on God, the atmosphere is set for something good to happen. Situations may not work out the way we wanted them to. Prayers may not be answered in the specific way we prayed for. But God is working in the waiting, and He always has a plan. We may not understand His ways at times. But trust that He is good. I had experienced great success in my EMDR and regular therapy. I had overcome so much pain from my past. Dr. Riedo was able to use her skills and training in order to help me get in alignment with my true self once more. Life was good, and that is where I needed to turn my focus.

And on Tuesday, October 20, 2020, I woke up and was committed to having a beautiful day. I began thanking God for His goodness. Gratitude will always breathe new life into you. I also woke up feeling like I needed to pray for David. Yes, my ex-husband David. When I arrived at work, I called David's office and asked him if he was busy and added that I would like to speak with him. David was good with it, so I went to his office. I told David that I felt like God wanted me to pray about three things for him. At that moment, I grabbed David's hand and started praying blessings over him. One of the specific things that I prayed about was that when the time came that David decided to tell Arica about the issue of Herpes, that he would not get rejected the way that I did. I honestly did not want him to experience that kind of pain. When I finished praying for David, he followed up by praying for me. His prayer for me was sweet and quite unexpected. But very welcomed. Then something happened that I would have never anticipated. David looked me in the eyes and apologized for the thing that had been a constant issue in our marriage. David apologized for putting ministry work before me. Anytime I had brought it up over the years, he denied it and got angry at me for even bringing it up. It was one of the main reasons that led to me finally filing for divorce. I could not compete with hundreds of other people. Sure, David and I had other issues, but this one issue was bigger than us. But David finally admitted it. He sincerely apologized for it. And I think that was the final resolution in a lifetime of hurt that I needed closure for. David and I talked for some time and apologized for a lot of things. We both needed that. It is amazing what God will do if you will just be obedient to Him. God told me to go and pray for my ex-husband, and it turned out to be a bigger blessing for me. For both of us, actually. God is good. Better than good.

I must follow this up by sharing something I believe is of immense importance. Just this past week, during my session with Dr. Riedo, we discussed David. She will often bring things up from my past just to make sure I really am healed from a traumatic incident. Dr. Riedo asked how David and his church were doing and how I felt about it all. I had no issue with telling her that David seems very happy and that I am very happy for him. I went on to share that I feel like God had been walking me further through healing. God and I were talking recently, and I feel as though I now understand David better. The fact that he put ministry before our marriage at times will never be "right." Andy Stanley wrote a book called "Choosing to Cheat." I did not read the book, but Andy was a guest on the television show I work for, and he discussed the book. The book is about establishing priorities and making choices within the work versus life balance. Andy spoke specifically about how pastors must learn to make the balance and not sacrifice their own families for other people's needs. It is challenging. I explained to Dr. Riedo that although many choices David made regarding ministry work hurt me over the years, I am not mad or hurt about it anymore. I went on to tell her that David had been trained up in the ministry since he was a pre-teen; he had been molded and prepared. It was his dream.

When David was offered the Senior Pastor position, and I asked him not to take it, and he did anyway, I think I understand why now. Our marriage was already falling apart. We were not "a sure thing." This job was. I am not excusing anything here. I am just acknowledging that I see things differently now. And if I had been in the same position, who is to say that I might not have done the same thing that David did. David and I both made a lot of mistakes in our marriage. But we exchanged apologies and are moving forward. The past is the past. The time that David and I talked that day at work brought healing we both needed.

Then one night, when Sofia and Lily were at David's, I was walking around the house and praying while blasting Praise and Worship music. I was listening to Bethel's "Raise a Hallelujah" when I stopped for a moment and had to sit down. All of the sudden, I heard the words, "You just kicked fear in the butt!" I didn't actually hear the word "butt," but if I wrote the word I did hear, people might say it wasn't from God. Either way, this statement brought great freedom to me. Why? I had faced the second biggest fear that I ever had to face. The first was when I had to tell my mom that I had been raped, was pregnant, and planning an abortion. The second, I had told someone that I had Herpes. I faced my fear. I was not destroyed. I was hurt. But I did the right thing. I was crushed. But I was not decimated. I honestly do not know who penned this quote, but it bears sharing again and again:

"The most free person in the world is the one who has nothing to hide."

All my "secrets" were out now. This doesn't mean I wanted to broadcast them on a billboard, although I am writing about them now. But my point is, I was free. Shame had lost its life-consuming stranglehold on me. And my thought was, "And if no man ever wants me, I might be sad, but I will be honest and free."

I want to make a strong point here. Never underestimate how your actions help form the thoughts of your children. I do love quotes. I write them on post-it notes and stick them on my computer, on my calendar, and on the mirror in my bathroom so I can see positive words as I am getting ready for the day. Consequently, one day I went into Sofia's room, and she had taken a dry erase marker and started writing positive quotes on her dresser mirror. BAM! YES! Your kids learn from you.

Back to the story. I was in a "good" place, but I was missing Freddy, so I had to put some extra positive "sayings" on my bathroom mirror, including the fact that I will honor and respect myself for the person God created me to be.

Dr. Riedo worked with me to help resolve the ending of the relationship with Freddy. She told me to make a list of the things I didn't like about him, little quirks or whatever, and concentrate on those. I told her there was absolutely nothing that I did not like about him. I believe she knew better considering her years of training, but she let it go for the time being. It was during this time that I really started contemplating writing this book. My life had been full of hills and valleys and heavily littered with trauma along the way. God had been instrumental in my healing process. He had exposed areas in which I did not even realize were trauma. God directed me to the perfect psychologist that would join with me to expose the darkness and the light. Medication played a role as well. But it got me to thinking, if I could help anyone else overcome a past that has kept them in a pit, a dark place, that's what I want to do. But did I really want people to know all my junk? Was I ready to completely expose my life?

For a time, I went back and forth about writing the book. The more I questioned the possibility, the more I would hear sermons or read something that reminded me that my life is not my own. Pastor Ed Young made a statement one time that stuck with me. He said that, "You are not ready to live until you are ready to die." He shared this as he was telling the congregation at Fellowship Church about the unexpected death of his daughter. But as Pastor Ed said these words, God spoke an additional line into my spirit, "You are not ready to live until you are ready to die…to self." I knew exactly what God was saying. My life, experiences, pain, trauma, healing, hope, redemption, joy aren't meant to be kept secret. If my story can help someone else, I must die to fear of what others might think of me and forge forward.

In addition to that encounter with God, suddenly, I felt like guests on the television show I work for spoke little nuggets of gold and inspiration God intended for me. Author and Founder of Mobilize Ministries Todd Lollar said, "Don't use your weakness as an excuse." My weakness had been fear.

Did I still want to let fear control me? Did I want the fear of abandonment and of people turning their backs on me and judging me to keep me from helping others if I could? One day I was listening to "Graves Into Gardens" by Elevation Worship. The song exemplifies God's goodness and speaks of how God can turn our shame into something glorious. Was I going to let my past shame or present potential for shame keep me hidden?

Author Kim Meeder was on our show telling a story of how she and her husband were out boating one day. The water became dangerous, and as they were heading back to the docks, they noticed an overturned boat. One man had already drowned, but Kim and her husband were able to save another man. Days later, that man called Kim and her husband to thank them, and he expressed to them, "I am alive because you stopped!" He told them how several other boats had passed by him and his friend's overturned boat, but he was alive because Kim and her husband didn't pass them by. So God decided to use a little play on words and extend what that man had said to Kim. In my head, I heard this, "I am alive because you stopped…thinking about yourself." If we quit worrying about what other people think, there is no limit to what God might achieve through us. How many people might you help? I believe this was God's way of telling me to get over it and trust Him.

According to author and pastor Toni Collier, "Hurt and hope can co-exist. Shame is the scheme of the enemy to hold us down mentally and emotionally from everything that God has for us on the other side of hope and healing. Shame is an identity snatcher. Thieves don't steal from empty houses. We all have something of value inside us." I had experienced much healing, and I have hope. Hope for today. Hope for tomorrow. Hope. I would love to help others get to that same place if I can. Someone once said that the true meaning of authentic is someone that is tried, found reliable, and completely qualified. I think I am somewhat qualified to help people see their worth that the enemy has blinded them to. I was then prompted to begin writing the outline for this book.

Luckily for David, when he told Arica about the diagnosis when they started dating, Arica is a nurse by training and knowledgeable on the facts about Herpes. She was secure in knowing that the virus is not life-threatening. Arica realizes that Herpes does not make you ill and that there are precautions that can be taken to lessen the chance of transmission. And luckily for me, on Sunday, November 8, 2020, when I woke up to get ready for church, I looked at my phone, and there were multiple messages from Freddy beginning at 4:54 am, the last one saying these sweet words, "I sure hope you have gave God time to work on my heart because it's all yours. I miss you so much. I hope it's not too late." My reply was, "It's never too late." I was overjoyed.

Dr. Riedo had already told me during a session that she personally did not think my relationship with Freddy was done with. Therefore, she was not the least bit surprised when I shared the news that Freddy and I had decided to reestablish our dating relationship. Freddy and I picked up where we left off. He was at peace with moving forward, and we began talking about a future together once more. We took great joy in discussing far-off places that we dreamed of traveling to. We had countless smiles and laughs as we explored adventurous ideas of items that were on each of our bucket lists. Freddy and I imagined retiring one day to a cabin in the woods and sitting on the porch drinking coffee as snow drifted and surrounded our peaceful home. Everyone needs dreams, and we had plenty to go around and work towards.

Thanksgiving Day of last year, 2020, was a big step for Freddy and me. We had made the decision that he would bring his boys and spend Thanksgiving with Sofia, Lily, and me. COVID was in full force. Both of our families had been diligent in taking precautions. Not one of us had any symptoms, so Freddy and I felt comfortable having our families spend the holiday together. I had never prepared a turkey before, but alas, I found an amazing recipe that I felt I could have success with. I was meticulous at formulating the menu, and my excitement could barely be contained. Thanksgiving Day was a huge success. Our kids were shy at first, but everyone warmed up to each other. Thank God all the food I had prepared proved to be quite yummy. Give me a good recipe, and I will give it my all. The six of us ate, talked, played games, and enjoyed the special day. After lunch, there was a trip to a local park for skateboarding and bike riding. That evening as we continuously snacked, we piled on the couch to watch a movie. It was a warm and special holiday. I was probably smiling from ear to ear. I thought this was my future. I thought wrong.

Freddy began to act "differently." I honestly could not put my finger on exactly what it was. When I questioned him about it, Freddy responded candidly that it was the distance thing again. He and I were both aware of the miles between us before we ever agreed to meet. I must admit that I was quite blind-sided when this issue became a problem again. We had both acknowledged that we could make it work. It was not working for him. I admit as well that it was difficult living so far apart when your true desire was to see the other person every day. It was hard when Freddy would call me from his kid's school and fill me in on the football game score. I wanted to be there. It was hard when I went to church, and I wanted him there with me. He was feeling the loss of not being able to experience life together. We both were. We were enduring being alone most of the time while being in this relationship. My hat honorably goes off for military personnel separated from their families for long periods of time. Or people that have spouses that work in the oil field and are gone for weeks at a time. You are made of true grit.

By Christmas, Freddy had blown me off again. I had no idea what was going on. I was hurt, again. Regardless, I had hired someone to make Freddy a special, personalized Christmas gift, and I decided to inform him that I was going to send him the gift. I wanted him to have it. Freddy sent me something as well. It was a sweet gift because he knew it was something I had talked about wanting.

By the beginning of 2021, Freddy was wanting back in my life. Freddy is an amazing human being. He, too, had experienced much trauma in his lifetime. From a murder that took place in his family to the loss of a child and multiple other incidents. I had told Freddy about my success with EMDR Therapy. I suggested that it might benefit him. I cared for Freddy, but I prayed about our situation and finally had to stand strong and just say no. I was reminded of all the things that Dr. Riedo had taught me about non-nego-tiables and the fact that I wanted an emotionally stable man in my life. I had worked hard, been in therapy for some time, and experienced such amazing healing and growth. I needed that same desire for wholeness and healing in whoever I was going to date. The fact that Freddy kept going back and forth about our relationship was a sign that something deeper might be going on with him. Freddy was showing too many red flags for me to be comfortable with. It was hard, but I had to let go. Freddy wanted to remain friends and keep talking in hopes that we could be together in the future when one of us could move closer to the other. The distance was no longer our only problem. I kindly expressed to Freddy that I could not in good conscience do that, and we just needed to end things. Dr. Riedo had been successful at teaching me to set boundaries in my life. Setting boundaries is not always easy, but the benefits outweigh the hardship.

Life has shown me that if you hold onto something that is not working, you might miss something right in front of you that could possibly work. I assure you I do not mean for that to sound odd or egotistical in any form or matter. I have just experienced too much to not know when to let go. And holding on to the past or "what might be" runs the chance of extinguishing what could be today. Live in the moment!

Currently, as I am writing this, it is May 2021. Freddy has contacted me twice in the last month. I have responded politely. It took me a lifetime to believe that God wants His best for me but now that I do believe that, in the words of Dr. Riedo, "Don't ever settle!" I want to be important to someone. I want to come first, after God, in someone's life. I want someone I can depend on. I want someone to be honest with me, even if it hurts. And I want to return that and even more for the man in my life. And I won't, I can't, settle for less. That's not arrogance. That is knowing God is good, and He wants only good for me.

I now need to refer back to a previous chapter. In the chapter regard-ing Herpes, I made reference to the fact that God is still in the business of healing people. And He is. Totally. Without a doubt. God physically healed Sofia and Lily. There is documented proof of both of those healings. God did not heal me of Herpes. At least, I don't think He has. I currently have no symptoms, but I have not been re-tested. No matter. What God did do was heal my heart. Freddy was instrumental in that process, and I will be forever grateful to him. Regardless that the relationship ended, I found out that a man could still care for me, want to be with me, plan a future with me, even after finding out I have Herpes. Unless you have walked in my shoes, you have no idea how huge that was for me to know. It was bigger than big. I thought I would be single for the rest of my life. I thought no man would ever want to be a part of my life or even consider marriage due to the Herpes diagnosis. I was wrong. A huge part of my heart has been restored, and my time with Freddy has given me hope for the future. I have complete faith in God that there is a man out there for me, and I will live the dream of getting married and growing old with someone. I trust my God!

I believe in love. I believe in marriage. I want to have someone to share life with, pray with, cook with, go on adventures with, do family times with, cry with, travel with, be creative with, go to church with, serve with, and love with. It's possible. I believe God will bring a man into my life that will love me for me…period. At the same time, if I remain single, then I will be okay as well. It is amazing what lessons we can learn in the ashes of life if we just open our eyes up to the beauty. Perspective.

"Life is not over when you think it is. You can't change your circum-stances, but you can be changed in the midst of your circumstances."

--Lecrae, Christian Hip Hop Recording Artist, Songwriter, Music Executive, Actor

"To know one's own heart is to know peace. To connect with another's soul is to know love."

--Julie D. Harper, Mom, Author, Producer, Dreamer, Overcomer

"There are only two ways to live your life. One is as if nothing is a miracle. The other is as though everything is a miracle."

--Albert Einstein

"See A Victory"

-By: Elevation Worship

"Rainbow"

-By: Kacey Musgraves

Chapter 22

Peace At Last
Sour Lemons? Make Sweet Lemonade

Remember in the "Introduction" of this book, I told you I had been asked the question, "If you could change one day in your life, would you?" Without hesitation, my reply was, "No." My answer was not one to be taken lightly, though. I have gone through some horrible, life-changing, mentally destroying things. I have been hurt. I have been abused. I have been abandoned by family and friends. I have dealt with depression. The list goes on. And I can assure you that I did not even mention everything I have endured in this book. But I refuse to be a victim. And if I changed one day in my life, I would not have Sofia and Lily. And my life has made me who I am. And I can honestly say that I am proud of who I am. Only God. Yes, only God could bring me from an existence of much despair to the actuality of me loving me. I am resilient. I am compassionate. I am a survivor. I am hopeful. I am healed. I am me, and there is no other person I would rather be. I want other people to experience the infilling of peace that is just waiting for them on the other side of whatever it is that broke them. I am a better mom because of what I have been through. Sofia and Lily will continue to grow up knowing they are loved, valued, priceless, beautiful, brilliant, and they matter. Not just to me but to God. I am closer to God because He never left my side, even when I could not feel Him there.

Sofia, Lily and I love going to movies. There is something about being at the theater with the smell of buttered popcorn, the amazing surround sound, the big screen, and lounge chairs. One evening as the three of us were leaving the theater and we got settled in the car, we began discussing the movie we had just watched. It was not a spiritual movie by any means, but I was amazed at all the spiritual innuendos within the movie. There was one line in the movie that was extremely thought-provoking. What it spoke to me was that it is the responsibility of those who are born strong to care for those that are weak. I believe this thought was spoken as an encouragement but also as a challenge.

God can use anyone and anything to speak to your spirit. I found myself asking God, "Am I strong? Was I born strong?" Because I certainly did not feel strong most of my life. In fact, it was just the opposite. I felt weak and helpless. But I am still here. I have persisted and pulled through everything that life has thrown at me. It was not easy. There were times it was gut-wrenching, unimaginably painful, and heartbreaking. There were days that I did not even want to get out of bed. There were times I believed the world would be better off without me. And worst of all, there were times that I cried until I could not even breathe. I am so glad that I did not give up. I am so glad that I held on. I am so glad God held me in my lowest points in life. I am so glad I held on to hope. I am so glad I can wake up in the morning with a smile on my face and start the day with gratitude and thanking God for another day. I have learned to forgive. Someone once said, "Unforgiveness is like drinking poison and expecting someone else to die." Was… I… Born… Strong? God didn't answer me, or maybe He answers me every morning when I wake up and look in the mirror. I am still here. And so are you.

"Don't be afraid to start all over again. You may like your new story better."

--Anonymous

"Remake your life in a way that works for you, and remake it now."

--Shauna Niequist, Author

Sofia, Lily, and I had Covid in January of this year (2021). If we had to have it, I am overly glad that we all had it at the same time. Lily had a headache for about three days, and then you could not even tell she was sick. She was bouncing off the walls, bored and mad that she could not go back to school for two weeks. Sofia felt sick for about three days as well. She was already participating in online school, so her life saw little change. I was tired and achy for about three days too. By tired and achy, I mean that I could not stay awake and felt like I had the flu. After the initial three days, I did feel better, although my ability to taste and smell was gone for two weeks. That was just weird. No other word for it. Weird. My biggest issue was my asthma. I was having major difficulty breathing. The situation was a bit scary. I made a call to my doctor, who decided to prescribe seven days of steroid treatment in order to keep my lungs clear.

On those days when it seemed like a struggle to take every single breath, I must come clean and admit that my mortality came into thought. People had died from Covid. I could die from Covid. Or have lingering health issues. What if I were to die? Would I have served my purpose on this earth? I told you, I am analytical and tend to think deep thoughts at times. I thought about my life. I thought about all I had been through. I thought about happy times. I thought about my kids. I thought about the goodness of God. And then, I thought about the people that might be struggling with some of the same challenges I had experienced in life. I thought about the people that felt helpless and hopeless. I thought about the people who had been abused. I thought about the women that had gone through abortion procedures. I thought about the people that had low self-worth. I thought about the people who had been beat up or disappointed by religion. I thought about the people who had considered suicide. I thought about the people who went through a divorce or lost a child. I thought about the people who have an "incurable disease." I thought about the prostitute that needs to know she is loved and has worth. I thought about people that have addictions to porn, drugs, alcohol, over-eating, and so forth as they wonder if they will ever feel in control again. I thought about the people in prison that want to taste freedom again. I was a prisoner in my mind. I fully realize that my situation was not the same as an inmate. However, mental and emotional distress or incapacity is a category of bondage. I have come a long way in the healing process. I will continue to heal throughout my life. Life will have struggles. But the struggles will not have me.

I am a fan of football (Go Cowboys! What? I live in the DFW Metroplex, y'all), and I have watched games for years. There is a former player that coined a phrase that I just adore. Terrell Owens would say, "I love me some me!" That phrase still makes me laugh, even today. Better yet, it makes me smile. I LOVE this simple quote. Maybe you just need to look in the mirror every day and say, "I love me some me!" What a way to start the day. You need to wake up every morning and look in the mirror and confidently say, "I love me some me!" You cannot truly love others well until you love yourself well first. Remember:

"And you must love the Lord your God with all your heart, all your soul, all your mind, and all your strength. The second is equally important: Love your neighbor as yourself. No other commandment is greater than these."

--Mark 12:30-31 (NLT)

So, in essence, we little earthly beings are actually commanded to love ourselves. It is not a selfish thing. It is a glorious thing. Now, I am not talking about being arrogant or egotistical. I am talking about looking at yourself and just knowing, just feeling, just accepting that you are fearfully and wonderfully made. You are not an accident. You are not worthless. You are not ugly. You are not stupid. You are you. And you are loved. You have a Father in heaven that crafted you with His very hands. He molded you. He perfected you. He made you in His own image. He loves you… just as you are… where you are at… this very moment… He loves you! You don't even have to believe in Him, and He still loves you. Psalm 24: 1 says this: "*The earth is the Lord's and everything in it. The world and all its people belong to Him.*"

(NLT) You are part of that "all." You are His. And He wants you to love you. I, of all people, know how hard that can be at times. Do not give up. Please listen to me. You are worth it.

I need to explain the deeper meaning of my decision to title this book the way that I did. When I started looking back on my life and the things that I had been through, I could now see Jesus every step of the way. His presence might not always have been clear to me, but He was there. Subsequently, I just could not see Him through the eyes of hurt, pain, neglect, abuse, alcohol, sex, depression. I have no idea why I went through some of the stuff that I went through. I am sure I could find plenty of people to blame, including myself. It really doesn't matter, though. What does matter is this: I am still here! I was not destroyed. I was not defeated. I lost some battles, but I won the war. And if you are still here, that should be a strong indication that you are not a loser; you are a warrior. And the battlefield is your mind. And Satan loves getting into your mind and filling it with all kinds of lies and blinding you to the truth and love of Christ. It really is just this simple:

"The light from the sun was gone. And suddenly, the curtain (veil) in the sanctuary of the Temple was torn down the middle."

--Luke 23:45 (NLT)

I am by no means saying what Christ suffered for us was simple. I am signifying the fact that His love for us was pure, unrelenting, passionate, sacred. This is what my NLT version of the Bible has to say about this passage of scripture: "*This significant event symbolizes Christ's work on the cross. The Temple had three parts: the courts for all the people; the Holy Place, where the high priest alone could enter once a year to atone for the sins of the people. It was The Most Holy Place that the Ark of the Covenant, and God's presence with it, rested. The curtain (veil) that was torn was the one that closed off The Most Holy Place from view. At Christ's death, the barrier between God and humanity was split in two. Now, all people can approach God directly through Christ.*" –**Life Application Study Bible NLT**

A veil is a type of covering. When something is unveiled, it exposes something. One might say that it reveals the truth or makes something visible. There were many, and I mean many, times I questioned God's love for me. I was blinded to what was right in front of me. I was fixated on my brokenness, and my perception of God was blurred. I was blinded by my emotions, and I have already expressed that your emotions will lie to you. For me, love is relentless, strong, immovable, unconditional, constant, intense, powerful, reliable devotion. I felt as though God had abandoned me. My "veil" had skewed me to God's love. Don't get me wrong, I have always known God loves me. But when your life is a tangled mess, you feel worthless. You don't feel the love. And that's not God's intention. That is the enemy that is bent on destroying you and everything good in your life.

"The Unveiling: A Place Where Pain & Passion Collide" is the story of my life. Just as when the curtain (veil) was split in two at the time of Christ's death in order to open up a direct pathway to God, the unveiling is when my pain collided with God's passion for me, and I started seeing truth. The truth of how much God abundantly loves me. I will never try to dismiss anyone's pain. Just know that God is holding you through it. Even if you can't feel it. God is there. He is with you in your darkest moments. Please hear this, God's fingerprints are all over my life. That is a truth that cannot be denied. That knowledge does not dismiss me from the fiery darts of the enemy. Satan is hell-bent on destroying every person that he can. My prayer to God is, "Lord, I give You my mind. Untangle the lies within, so all I hear is Your truth." God is our defender. He is waiting on our call for help.

Once again, I highly recommend EMDR Therapy to every single person that has experienced trauma in their life. Sometimes we need help to clear the muddy waters in our mind and see, feel, know the truth. And the truth is, you are amazingly and exponentially loved!

I am now going to ask you to do something. I can't ask you to close your eyes or you could not read this, but as you read, I hope you can get a vision in your mind as I write. Imagine waking up one morning and knowing exactly what the day had in store. You are broken. You are hated. You are a prisoner. People you thought you could trust turned their backs on you. You feel like you are carrying the weight of the world on your shoulders. You are shamed. You are beaten down. You are bruised. You are bloody. Your strength is gone. You are spit on. You are cursed at. You are mocked. You are put on display. You are struggling…until the struggle is over. Or is it?

"Jesus said, 'Father, forgive them, for they don't know what they are doing.'"

--Luke 23:34 (NLT)

"Jesus called out with a loud voice, 'Father, into your hands I commit my spirit.' When he had said this, he breathed his last."

--Luke 23:46 (NIV)

If you have never seen the movie "The Passion of The Christ," I highly recommend it. It is not for the faint of heart. You feel like you are there, in person, witnessing the brutal death of Christ. But it is not the end of the story. It is the beginning. When Jesus gave His life for you and me, He did it willingly. He suffered much for us because of His relentless love for us. His death brought us life. His resurrection gives us hope. His love is immeasurable. Allow your eyes to be unveiled. See yourself as the magnificent creation that God crafted you to be. There is absolutely nothing in your life that disqualifies you from the love of Christ. You are amazing. You are fearfully and wonderfully made. A few years back, when I was still struggling with, well, me, I heard the Lord say to me so lovingly and graciously:

"Quit trying to be and just be."

-From God To Me (June 2018)

What? Is my life really that non-complex, effortless, uncomplicated, easy? Okay, maybe I should not overdo what I am trying to say here. I have already mentioned that life has struggles, and that is true. But I believe what God was trying to convey to me at that moment was to quit trying to live up to everyone else's expectations, including my own. Do you know how freeing that is? Don't let the lies in your head destroy you. Don't let your battered emotions manipulate you into being someone you're not or saying or doing things you know you shouldn't. Don't let the opinions of others steal your life force. And don't try to heal on your own. Everyone needs someone. And a lot of us need professional help to overcome certain issues. There is no shame in that.

And just as in the scripture references above, I think we need to use Jesus as the example and start with forgiving. Whether you need to forgive someone else or yourself, forgiveness is the perfect starting place. And then, give it to God. God will give you the wisdom to take the steps you need in order to find hope and healing. Please don't think you can do this on your own because you can't. You can be a positive prayer warrior and a fasting fool (that is directed at me because I thought that was all I needed), but most people honestly need more than that. And that's okay. And I will just be honest; some counselors are not qualified to deal with some issues. I made sure I found a psychologist that was trained in EMDR Therapy. At the same time, please do not think I am a therapy pusher. I just know what worked for me. Once you get your mind and thoughts working properly, it is possible for you to see your life from a whole new perspective. Your perspective has the power to determine where your life is going. I pray you have a grand perspective. Every single day of our lives, we are presented with choices, with decisions to make. Our response to those choices and decisions is what makes up our lives. If you ever want to see how this is magnificently demonstrated, you should read a book called "The Butterfly Effect" by Andy Andrews. It could change how you see your life.

I felt I would share some more quotes and suggest some more happy, happy music for your soul:

"Retrain your brain to reframe your pain."

-Ben Courson, Senior Pastor at Applegate Christian Fellowship, Author, TV and Radio Personality, International Speaker, Founder of Hope Generation

"Just breathe. Keep your eyes on God. That's all. No other expectations. Just breathe. And you will come through."

-Written to American pastor Andrew Brunson as he awaited trial in a Turkish prison

"God's Not Done With You"

-By: Tauren Wells

"Way Maker"

-By: LeeLand

"Priceless"

-By: For King and Country

"Beloved"

-By: Jordan Feliz

Chapter 23

Bringing It All Together
The Choice Is Yours

Right about now, it probably seems like I should be wrapping up this book. The last chapter could have made for good closure, but I truly do sense that I need to share a few more things. In my perception, there may be more details that might be helpful for some of you reading this. Hence, I did not want to leave these elements out of my story.

I started this book, in the "Introduction," with a quote from Pastor Tony Evans. I believe it bears repeating:

"If all you see is what you see, you will never see all there is to be seen."

Can I get an amen, or high five, or both? You have been invited in to experience my life throughout the pages of this book…the good, the bad, the beautiful, the ugly, the heartbreak, the redemption, the sadness, and the ultimate joy. I deem it would not be appropriate or fair for me to leave loose ends regarding the people in my life. Specifically, I do not want to conclude this book without clarifying a few relationships. In other words, I want to unravel any ideas that might have left any bad impressions of particular people that were mentioned in this book.

I want to begin with my dad. Happily, I can report that my dad is a healthy and hard-working 80-year-old-farmer. Dad's greatest joys are being on a tractor, bringing in a harvest, feeding his cows, and eating tons of fried food. Even so, he is pretty much in good health. My mom fusses at him all the time. I tell her to let him be. If dad dies in a field cutting hay, that is how he would want to go.

My dad was not very present in my life. Or in the lives of my brothers. For the first half of my life, I did not understand this type of a relationship. And it hurt me. I think our interactions, or lack of, made me feel unwanted. Truth be told, I had always heard the story of how my dad communicated to my mom that they would not stop having children until they had a girl. My mom was incredibly happy when number four…that would be me… came along. Consequently, mom immediately had her tubes tied. I know my dad loved me. Better yet, he loves me. But I needed more from him. I do not judge or fault him. In fact, in the years that I have been working as a television producer and hearing other people's stories, I think I finally "understand" my dad.

Pastor Jimmy Evans of Gateway Church in Southlake, Texas, once shared a story about his father. I will share the main details, but the entire incident is worth looking into. Jimmy never had a great relationship with his dad. It hurt Jimmy and left a scar that his dad did not attend his games and so much more. His dad utterly worked all the time and missed much of Jimmy's growing-up years. It wasn't until Jimmy was older that he found out that his dad's method of expressing love was by providing for his family. That explained the reasoning that Jimmy's dad worked all the time and missed so many family events. When Jimmy discovered this bit of information, it changed everything for him because his perspective of his dad changed. Jimmy then knew undoubtedly how much his dad loved him, even if his dad was absent from Jimmy's games.

Jimmy's story helped me to understand my own dad better. My dad, too, was a workaholic. At the same time, dad had a family of six to provide for. That is a pressure I did not understand as a child. But I do now that I am a parent. Probably even more so now that I am a single mom and the primary provider for Sofia, Lily, and all the bills that come due every month. My dad has shown me countless means of love. My eyes and heart just did not see it at the time. But now, the veil has been lifted, and I see the truth clearly. My dad is awesome!

While we are on the subject about dad's, I feel as though it might be beneficial to submit a bit of information here. Again, I am blessed to meet many amazing individuals in my role as a television producer. Throughout the years, our program has had the honor of hosting numerous psychologists and counselors as guests. I have heard time and again that little boys get their identity from their mothers while little girls get their identity from their fathers. I do not recall the data on this information. The only reason I bring this up is I was a little girl, and I searched for my identity, and it took me down an ugly road. I needed a strong male figure to affirm me. What I want to discuss currently here is the subject of fatherlessness. This topic is a growing epidemic in not only our country but around the world. Obviously, I am not a man; therefore, I feel that I do not have the authority to address this issue. But I will tell you what Pastor Tony Evans recently said about it as he was a guest on our show to discuss his most recent book "*Kingdom Men Rising.*"

"God did not create Adam and Eve at the same time. He created Adam first. Gave Adam His responsibility. Gave Adam His word. Because God holds men responsible first. When men abandon their lead responsibility, women are critical...they're essential. She's an essential collaborator. But when mankind fell, God didn't come and say, 'Adam and Eve, where are y'all.' He said, 'Adam, where are you?' The Bible says, 'And Adam died.' Not 'and Adam and Eve died.' When God did the covenant, He said, 'I'm the God of Abraham, Isaac, and Jacob.' Not 'Sarah, Rebekah, and Rachael.' In other words, He would hold men ultimately responsible. In Exodus Chapter 34 verse 23, God called all the males, He left all the women home, and He said, 'If I can get you men to listen to Me, I will send you back, and I'll save your nation.' So, He holds men ultimately responsible. So, when

men fail, it's like the foundation of a house failing. The other parts are critical, but the stability of the parts is dependent upon the solid foundation. Foundations don't have to be pretty, but they better be strong. So, God is calling men to be strong so that everything else, families, churches, and culture, can be built on their strength. Because, if not, then we're calling on women to be women and men. And God is not calling on them to be both. He's calling us to be men. The Bible says in Isaiah chapter 3 that when men fail, 'The children rebel, the women take over, and the men become weak.' So, the Bible holds men ultimately responsible. The first thing men need to understand is that the culture can no longer define us. The culture has taken us in two different directions; both are wrong. Turned us into passive leaders so that, like Adam, we're sitting there listening to the devil talking to our mates while we keep quiet. So that's passive leadership. Then there's the other side where there's this dominating, oppressive definition of manhood. Both are non-Biblical extremes that the culture gets us wrapped up in because we lose a Kingdom mindset. And a Kingdom man is defined as a male who comes under divine accountability and responsibility. So, I'm trying to get people to think Kingdom in defining their manhood and their maleness and not culture. So that's the challenge of rejecting the culture and submitting ourselves to a Biblical worldview because everything else is dependent upon it."

If you are wondering the reasoning behind me bringing all of this up, my answer is simplistic. I did not have a strong male figure in my life as a little girl to give me my identity. That crucial need in my mental development was missing…absent from my life. I have already expressed that I now understand why my dad was not around much during my childhood years. Dad and I now have a wonderful relationship. But, as a child, I felt ugly and unwanted. And eventually, it did cause me to rebel. I am certainly not going to use that as an excuse for some decisions I made, but it certainly did contribute to my unstable state of mind. Therefore, if you have been through a similar upbringing, whether you are a man or woman, I want you to reanalyze some areas of your life. And if your mom or your dad was not present in your life to affirm you, please do not allow this to make you question how amazing you are. Never allow the enemy into your mind like that and make you feel like you are ugly, unwanted, undeserving, or worthless. You have a Father in heaven that formed and created you, and He loves you beyond measure. Go to the Bible and read all the amazing things God has to say about you. You truly are the apple of His eye. You are worthy. You are loved.

Now let us proceed further and discuss my relationship with my mom. Without question, there were obvious issues in our relationship during my childhood and teenage years. There is a good chance that a part of the population could proclaim the same in their parent/child relationship. But now that I look back and realize some huge truths regarding my mom, I can see why some issues between us were the way that they were. My mom did not have a close relationship with her mother. That alone explains much. Our parents are our number one role models. Mom had a difficult childhood, moving many times, working the cotton fields, and her family was poor in her early years. She is a twin herself, and she had twin brothers that died. Well, one was stillborn, and the other died shortly after birth. I believe that my mom was overwhelmed with being a mom and serving almost as a single parent to four children ages 6 and under. My dad was not available to help my mom. I believe my mom was overburdened.

In recent years, I have been told by doctors that depression can be inherited. I deal with depression, and I believe my mom dealt with depression. Mom was never diagnosed due to the fact she never sought help like I did. She most likely never even considered depression being an issue in her life. I know that mom had challenges with substance abuse at one point. I thoroughly understand that. Alcohol was my substance of choice in order to try and numb my pain and forget the past. And Mom has dealt with some loss in her life. I now see that she was a fragile person that did not have the support that she desperately needed. I honestly believe mom did the best she could and made the decisions she thought were right. Mom has admitted that she made some mistakes. And for that alone, she is an honorable person in my book. My mom and I have a close and wonderful relationship.

As I have been going through my healing journey, a few years ago I asked my parents if I could speak with them in private. I teared up as I asked them for their forgiveness. They both asked, "For what?" I explained that I knew that I had made some wrong decisions when I was younger and that I probably hurt them numerous times and I needed their forgiveness. Their reply was sweet and almost made me laugh. They both said, "You were the least of our problems." Closure.

My oldest brother Vance is still an alcoholic to this day. Instead of judging him, though, I have compassion for him. It saddens me to see how this substance has taken over his life. Vance is frail and has multiple health issues, as you can imagine. There was a time I felt like I hated him for being so mean to me. I now understand that something must have happened to him to send him down the debilitating road of substance abuse. What broke him? What made him give up hope? What pain could he just not deal with? What difficulty transpired in his life? I do not know the answers to these questions. But I also requested a private conversation with him several years back. I brought up our childhood, and I told him that I felt like I had hated him, and I needed to ask for his forgiveness. We both teared up. Vance and I had a deep, personal conversation. He admitted to his misconduct. We forgave each other. My brother and I sealed it all with a hug.

I did not get the opportunity to make things right with David's mom, Joyce, before she passed away from cancer. I will get that chance when I see her again on the other side of this existence. Then again, I honestly don't think it will even matter then. It would not surprise me at all if we met each other with a big hug. Our differences did not have the power to kill love. And we did love each other. Joyce and I will have our day. But my point to you is, please do not wait. You never know when you may no longer have the chance, the time, the opportunity to make things right with people. Even if you may not have been the person "in the wrong," forgiveness brings freedom. It might not bring resolution or even be received by the other person or persons involved. Regardless, it's worth it. Do not let unforgiveness rob you of any more of your life. You need to breathe freely once more. Let that weight go.

David and I are at peace with one another. That is a very good place for us to be. We are co-parenting and raising Sofia and Lily to the best of our abilities. I understand that every divorce is different. Circumstances that lead to divorces are different. David and I resolved that although our marriage did not last, our parenting must last. We made the choice to respect each other and get along. If not for our sake, then for Sofia's and Lily's. David and I legitimately co-parent quite well. We talk multiple times a week and share certain expenses for Sofia and Lily. I have had to ask David to help me drop my car off to get worked on. He has asked to borrow tools from me. We genuinely respect each other and help each other in any way we can. And David's church is doing wonderfully well and growing.

Arica and I reconciled our differences, and I honestly have no ill feelings towards her. There has been much forgiveness in our little circle. By the time this book is published, David and Arica will be married and living four doors down from me. Our determination to live in peace does not mean there will never be issues between us; that's part of life. But we do not let the issues overtake us. And in situations like ours, you often must set boundaries. Especially where parenting and step-parenting is concerned. And that's okay. In fact, boundaries are needed. I know friends that do not share the same success story after a divorce. I am blessed that David, Arica, me, and all our kids and grandkids get along. It does make life much more enjoyable. We all had to do our part to make it happen.

In the big scheme of life, there was one last person I needed to ask for forgiveness from. And no, it's not God. I apologize to Him daily for one thing or another. He is a good Father. He listens, and we move on. But it was imperative that I forgave me. Executing such a challenge proved difficult at times. In order to move forward in life, it was not an option. I had forgiven so many other people from my past, but it wasn't until I forgave me that I actually started liking me. Our minds can get so clouded by the judgments of other people, culture, not feeling like we measure up to what we see on TV and social media, religious mindsets, not receiving the nurturing we desperately needed when we were children, and so many other things. It's time for the clouds to clear and for the beauty of life to shine through. Forgive you. I do not see forgiveness as a choice, yet an obligation. Receive your own forgiveness. And love you. You are worth it!

I have been searching for the perfect location to place this next statement into the book. There is no better time like the present. Are you ready? Can you get tuned in? This is paramount. If you get absolutely nothing else from this book, I want you to hear this loud and clear and realize it: GOD HAS NEVER FAILED ME! I am here. I am forgiven. I am happy. I am blessed. I am loved. I am beautiful (that one is hard to feel at times, but we are all works of art). I am a work in progress. I am healed (and that will be an ongoing process as life is always throwing something at us). I am strong. I am not a victim. I am a victor. And so are you. You need to remember; you have the power, grit, and determination within you to do your part. You are an essential element in your healing, your restoration, your life.

I know there are times that God heals a person instantly. I have seen it in my own family life. I have seen God deliver some people from an addiction in a moment. I have a dear friend that smoked two packs of cigarettes a day, and God set her free from that bondage instantaneously. I have witnessed many situations such as this. But these events are not as common as we would like them to be. I had to admit I had a problem. I had to confess that my emotions were overtaking me. I had to want to get better. I had to take the time to research and make calls and find an amazing psychologist. I had to pray. Over the years, I had to walk away from some friendships that were not beneficial to me. I had to quit going to bars and dance clubs when I was in my 20s. I had to move to another state at one point. I had to learn to control my emotions to some extent. I had to forgive. I had to accept some stuff that I did not want to have to accept. I had to trust God. I had to focus more on the moment and what I wanted for my future instead of the mistakes and pain of the past. I had to change my perspective. And I cried and screamed a lot along the way. A lot. Trust me. Buy yourself a good, thick pillow and scream into it until the emptiness inside is gone. Even if just for a moment. All of the tactics I had to do were worth it. No one can do these things for you. The power of choice is in your hands. Who knows what beauty is on the other side of the veil that has been hiding the real you all these years?

I spoke of "identity" and "choice" in this chapter, so as it would be me, I take great joy in sharing with you more spirit-raising, thought-provoking, remarkable quotes and songs that have put inspiration in my heart:

"We perceive we are rejected, and that's Satan's greatest tool. He steals our identity."

--Bobby Petrocelli, Author, Speaker, Coach

"The thing that scares Satan the most is a Christian who really believes in who they are."

--Anonymous

"Give who you are. The world will be a better place for it."

--Annie Downs, Author, Speaker

"But like bugs in a jar, we can't hope to shine if we're captive to a lesser way of life. The only way to shine brightly is to take flight, to be fully and freely who we were made to be."

--Michele Cushatt, Author, Speaker

"You are a choice away from a new beginning."

--Trent Shelton, Former Football Athlete, Author, Speaker, Founder of "Rehab Time"

"Whether you think you can, or you think you can't—you're right."

--Henry Ford, American Auto Maker

"Overcomer"

--By: Mandisa

"Who Says?"

--By: Joshua Micah

"Gotta Live"

--By: Tedashii with Jordan Feliz

"Speak Life"

--By: Toby Mac

"My Testimony"

--By: Elevation Worship

One last thought before I end this chapter. I must admit that I do not watch tons of television. Maybe this is due to the fact that I work in television or maybe it could be that I am a little busy bee and can always find something to do. "Boredom" is not even part of my vocabulary. My sweet young Lily is fascinated with anything medical though, and she dreams of being a veterinarian one day. Lily enjoys watching "Dr. Pimple Popper" with her dad. I really find it hard to stomach those videos, so thank God David can facilitate that desire in Lily. Lily loves to cuddle up on the couch as she and I watch television shows that involve any type of medical need. Her favorites are Chicago Med, Chicago Fire, Rescue 911, and Rescue 911 Lonestar. Lily has a heart for people, and she is very nurturing and always willing to lend a helping hand. I believe that is what touches her heart about these television shows. Lily wants to be part of the "rescue" one day.

Another show we have a ball watching is America's Got Talent. The show is encouraging, funny, fascinating, and it feels wonderful to glimpse the participants' dreams coming true. Recently a woman named Jane, who goes by the stage name "Nightbirde," auditioned for the show. Her audition went viral. You can check it out on YouTube. She wrote and performed a song titled "It's Okay." Jane said the song was about her previous year, battling cancer. Jane is physically beautiful, but her inner beauty is what captured the hearts of the audience and the judges. Jane shared that she has been given a 2% survival rate. She smiled and stated that 2% is better than 0%. What a fighter! Jane made two comments that really moved me. She said, *"I'm so much more than the bad things that happen to me,"* and *"You can't wait for things to get better to be happy."* I believe everyone around the world watching her audition witnessed her flight that night. Her perspective about her life, her challenges, her disease was coming from her heart. Not her head. Jane could sit down and give up if she allowed her mind to tell her it's all just too hard. But Jane looks at life from her heart and sees the life and beauty all around. What an amazing woman and a perfect example of taking life for all it has to offer.

Chapter 24

Ugly Is The New Beautiful

This chapter goes out to all you women and men who have ever felt ugly. You know, unattractive. Yes, I said it because that is the way I felt a big part of my life. It seemingly does not matter how many times other people tell you that you are pretty or handsome; if you don't feel it, you don't feel it. That being said, I do not want you to just feel it. I want you to own it. Now I am not talking about being egotistical, ugh, no. I am speaking about a perception that makes you feel, WOW! There is a song by Meghan Trainor called "Me Too." This song invariably makes Sofia, Lily, and me laugh, sing out loud, and want to dance around the room. Why? Because music moves us. Music is powerful. Before I go any further, you really should go online and listen to the song. Or just feel free to read on.

Some people may not believe in the importance of specific things I am about to say, but I sincerely hope you take these thoughts to heart. My kids can vouch for what I am about to share. This situation happens mostly when my kids and I are in the car, but it happens at home as well. Sofia, at 15 years old, now has her driver's permit. She wants to drive whenever the opportunity arises. Sofia takes great joy in connecting her phone to my car so she can listen to her playlist of songs. And no, Sofia is not allowed to mess with her phone while she is driving. Upon getting settled within my car, I say this phrase to her, often, "I do not want to hear any I'm lonely, I'm depressed, I suck, the world sucks, stick a fork in my eye songs." I usually get an eye roll, but she knows exactly what I am talking about. Sofia and Lily have played songs for me that literally make me want to dig a pit and jump in it and never come out. Actually, I would not jump in a pit. But I hope you know what I am communicating here. There are times I will go online and look up the lyrics of the songs the girls have played for me. The songs are actually even more depressing than I had originally thought.

People, please listen to me; music is powerful. Music can make you kick up your heels and want to dance around the house. Or, it can make you think your life isn't worth living. I am not trying to be offensive here in any way. I am not trying to be disrespectful to any musical artists. But what I am noting here is the truth. I will be brutally honest here; if I hear certain songs, they bring me hope. Some songs make me want to dance. Other songs put sexual thoughts into my head. Some send me into praise and worship. And then there are those songs that can make me completely depressed and put me in a dark place. I choose not to listen to such songs.

Turn the station, please. Music affects your spirit and your emotions and mindsets. You should be very careful of what you are inviting into your mind through music and song. I love music. I do. But you should take music seriously and be sensitive to what you are filling your head with. I listen to probably 70% Christian music because it is uplifting to me. And the Christian music I listen to is not the stuff I heard in church as a kid. Again, I am not trying to be offensive. I like some of the old hymns. But I like the new stuff much better. That's just me. I listen to Air 1 radio station all the time. I often wake up with Dan and Michelle (the morning DJs) making me laugh prior to a great song coming on as I am beginning my day and slapping on some make-up. The world is a better place when I have on make-up. Trust me.

I have mentioned specific songs throughout this book that literally changed my life, filled me with hope, instilled peace in me, and brought me into the presence of God. I also listen to modern pop music and have many artists that I am so glad are using the gifts that God gave them. I have been known to dance around the kitchen when BTS "Dynamite" is playing. Just saying. And when I need a little boost of energy, I might ask Alexa to play "Confident" by Demi Lovato. My whole point is, listen to uplifting, fun, positive music if you want to be happy, motivated, and positive. That's all. Well, Justin Timberlake's "Can't Stop The Feeling" will get our house dancing too.

At times in my life where I have just felt weak, beaten up, and alone, I have often turned to quotes, scriptures, and positive affirmations to inspire me and put some hop back into my step. As I had mentioned in a previous chapter, Sofia, Lily, and I write on one another's mirrors to show our love towards one another. I have scriptures and quotes posted on my bathroom mirror and right here beside my desk at home…eye-level, so there is always an encouraging word near me. I have things posted on the kitchen refrigerator as well. I like food, so I go to the refrigerator often. So this is a good place for positive words to flow.

When King David was on the run for his life, we are told that he encouraged himself in the Lord. That comes from 1 Samuel 30:6. No one else was going to lift David's spirit or tell him some good news. He was being hunted. He knew there was a chance that he could be murdered. It was just him and God. There may be times in life when you are the only person around to encourage you. Do it! Speak positive words out loud. It becomes even more real when you hear your own voice saying good things about you or to you.

I walk around the house reading scriptures out loud during times of great need or when I just want to praise God. I have positive artwork all around my house. One of my favorite stores in the whole wide world is Hobby Lobby. You can always find great stuff there. Right now, as I am sitting at my desk, this is what the multiple pieces of artwork in my office says: "Be The Exception," "Stay Humble, Work Hard, Be Kind," "365 New Days, 365 New Chances," "Your Dreams Don't Work Unless You Do," "It's A Good Day To Have a Good Day," "I Can Do All Things Through Christ Who Gives Me Strength -Philippians 4:13," "You Are So Loved," and "Stay Positive, Work Hard, Make It Happen." Okay, you should be in a good mood just reading those. There is inspirational, affirming artwork and quotes like that all over my house. Why? Because I am human and need constant reminders. Period. I also have lovely artwork by Sofia and Lily on my walls. That always adds a little extra smile to my day. My baby girls rock!

Another way to shake off the "ugly" in life and make it beautiful is to get outside yourself. Focusing on your own problems is needed, but sometimes you need a vacation from your issues. In the Spring of 2020, when my kids never returned to school after Spring Break due to Covid, the kids were getting restless, so we decided to bless other people. We knew if we were tired of being cooped up, then there had to be other people just like us. I went online and asked anyone who needed cheering up to send us their address. Sofia and Lily colored pictures, and we all signed cards and mailed out little packets of happiness and cheer. This little undertaking had Sofia and Lily laughing, coloring, writing, and even asking about the people that sent us their addresses. It was a totally fun experience. I tell Sofia and Lily that God blesses us so that we can be a blessing to others. Do nice gestures without expecting anything in return. God knows your heart, and He sees. And wouldn't you know it, my friend from childhood, Kim, saw what Sofia and Lily were doing for others and surprised them by sending them a care package. There were all kinds of cool gifts for Sofia and Lily. Thanks, Kim, for showing my girls that nothing goes unnoticed by God. You blessed Sofia and Lily.

Another time during the 2020 Covid lockdown, I put on my mask, and I made a quick journey up to Home Depot. I loaded the trunk of my car with potted flowers. These were delightful flowers of red, yellow, orange, and pink. Sofia, Lily, and I borrowed my neighbor's golf cart (Thanks, Betsy), drove around our neighborhood, and put the potted flowers on people's front porches. We didn't ring doorbells. We just dropped off the flowers and left. Then on to the next house we went. Sofia and Lily loved it. The recipients loved it. Win! Win! But we were the ones truly blessed through the experience, and Sofia and Lily got to learn about giving back. When we focus on others, we naturally forget about our own issues, if only for a little while. Blessing others can change your perspective and make you realize just how blessed you are. I love to bake. There are times I feel led to make a variety of cookies, bread, or candy and take the goodies to friends and neighbors. This is an inexpensive way to make people feel thought of and special.

Another thing I personally did in 2020 was to accomplish something that God had put on my heart a year or two earlier, but I never felt like the timing was right. The timing became right. I was at work one day, and I just knew I could start this little project. I picked 15 people from the course of my life to write gratitude letters to. I knew the exact 15 people that I intended to write to. These were people that had made a positive impact on my life at one point or another…in one way or another. Some of the recipients included my parents, David, Sofia and Lily, friends, Dr. Riedo and even Freddy. I might mention that the writing of these letters took place during an extremely difficult period of my life, but it helped me to stay focused on positivity. I did this with no expectation or "need" to hear back from these people. Most of the individuals are still a part of my life. My spirit was touched as the response was heart-warming. Even when you are in a tough spot in life, you never know how God might use you to bless someone else that needs a simple encouraging word. Sometimes the people that we see as "strong" are often the loneliest and in need of a hug or simple note of affirmation.

Always remember that you are a work of art. You are. God formed and molded you. Regardless of the issues you must work on throughout life, in God's eyes, you're perfect. You're beautiful. This song is not a Christian song, but it speaks much truth.

"Perfect"

--by: Pink

I could not end this chapter without sharing a most beautiful truth of God's love:

"…to bestow on them a crown of beauty instead of ashes, the oil of joy instead of mourning, and a garment of praise instead of a spirit of despair."

-Isaiah 61:3 (NIV)

Chapter 25

The Three Kinds Of Trauma
Time To Heal

Trauma often begins in childhood but can take place at any time throughout life. As a result, trauma can manipulate your thoughts and how you view yourself and others. Even though things like physical abuse takes place as an attack on our bodies, the trauma takes place in our minds. Trauma can cause various complications in a person's life and can even go as far as giving rise to identity issues. I am sure you have heard, "I think therefore I am." Our core beliefs about ourselves turn into our actions. The world has forced us to deal with things. Some things that we are not prepared to deal with. As humans, we are more anxious than we have ever been. Some people are more isolated than they have ever been. In the dark recesses of our minds, trauma may be lurking and patiently waiting to cause great turmoil in our lives. Trauma can incite negative reactions to things and people in your life, and you may not even know it's taking place. I do not use that as an excuse for any past behavior in my life. But at least now I know what the root issue was, and I now have the insights on how to overcome the trauma from my past and respond appropriately to situations presented in my life. There is no reason to sugar-coat it; if you have experienced trauma in your life, you most likely will not get over it on your own. There will be days you feel as though you are on top of the world. And you are. But the lasting ramifications normally associated with trauma do not just go away and will continue to affect your life…if you let it.

Subsequently, there may be things you experienced in life that you do not even realize are trauma. Trauma seems like such a technical word that means something "big" must have happened to you. Trauma comes in all shapes, sizes, and intensities. There are basically three main classifications of trauma: acute, chronic, or complex.

Acute trauma is the result of a single incident like the loss of a child, a rape, an abortion, the end of a relationship, an unsuccessful surgery, a serious car wreck, or a harsh word spoken that kills every sense of self-worth in your life. After my divorce, when I felt like many individuals turned their backs on me, that was a traumatic experience. Your body can internalize the pain and cause unhealthy behavior. Trauma can cause you to act in certain ways you normally would not. Trauma can indeed have that manner of power over you.

Chronic trauma is trauma that is repeated or prolonged for a period of time, such as domestic violence, abuse of any sort, and yes, verbal abuse can cause trauma. If another human being constantly demeans or threatens you in any way, that is verbal abuse, and it can cause lifelong issues in your life. Also, I have read stories of parents withholding food from children as a disciplinary punishment. This action would be trauma imposed on a child, and there is absolutely nothing right about it.

Complex trauma is when you are exposed to multiple traumatic events varying in nature. These events often take place in an invasive and inter-personal way. Complex trauma usually begins in childhood, but this is not always the case. Examples of complex trauma would be ongoing physical, emotional, or sexual abuse as well as neglect and abandonment. This type of trauma is associated as well when a child witnesses ongoing abusive behavior inflicted on someone else, such as a parent or sibling. Severe emotional trauma is more serious than most people might even think. In studies, severe emotional trauma causes lasting changes in the ventromedial prefrontal cortex region of the brain. This part of the brain is responsible for regulating emotional responses, how you respond to trauma, triggered by the amygdala. Remember when I discussed the Fight, Flight, or Freeze response in an earlier chapter? Well, the amygdala is your brain's safety regulator, and it is what activates the Fight, Flight, or Freeze response in your body. To be more specific, this area of the brain manages negative emotions, such as fear or anxiety, that transpire when a person is confronted with specific stimuli. If any of this sounds like you, there is help. Trauma can be treated. Your brain can be, in a sense, reprogrammed in order for you to move past the trauma. This is possible whether the trauma happened two days ago or occurred fifty years ago.

God still does the miraculous, but more often, we need help in dealing with trauma. EMDR Therapy changed my life. I cannot even begin to imagine where I would be at in life right now had I not sought help. For those of you who do not have health insurance that covers therapy, there are other options. Some government and private agencies offer programs for therapy. I know of churches that offer free counseling, but most times, you need to be a member of that church. You do have options, though, and searching for ways to find help will be worth it. I do advise that you do your research. When I was looking for a psychologist, I did extensive reading of reviews and visited the websites of multiple therapists before going with the doctor that I made an appointment with. Dr. Riedo applied her skills as a trained doctor in order to help me face my past, enjoy my present, and look forward to the future. This book does not offer you a formula on how to better your life. Every person is different. Every trauma is different. Every healing is different. I have shared what worked for me. You can find what works for you. Never doubt that God's gift of grace was instrumental in me finding my way through the darkness. God was with me every step of the way to cheer me on and to tell me when I needed to make some things right before I could move further ahead.

If you need prayer or an encouraging word, many ministries, churches, and Christian radio stations have prayer centers or prayer lines. The television show that I currently work for has an entire staff of people that take phone calls all day long to pray with those in need. Just don't give up. Keep fighting. Again, you are so worth it. Believe it. You need to take the first step towards finding healing. You can do this. You need to experience reconciliation with your past in order to walk into an emotionally healthy future. Set a vision for how you want your life to be. You have to see it before you see it. Start somewhere. Get your fight back. When my mind tries to take me to a place of negative thoughts, I fight back. I pray. I read my Bible. I speak positive words of affirmations. I listen to music that reminds me that I was not made for defeat. There is a song that was used in NBC promos for the 2018 Winter Olympics. The song is a confirmation that I was made for so much more.

"Made For This"

-By: Carrollton

Chapter 26

Finally Famous
Winners And Losers: You Win

My ex-husband David used to say something that has always stuck with me. I don't recall where he said he had heard this saying, but it is worth remembering and repeating. It is simply this, "Your opinion of me is none of my business." You may need to go back and read that again. Basically, it is saying that we should not allow the opinions of others to dull our light. You, me, we all have an audience of One, and to Him, you are the apple of His eye. God's opinion is the only one you should care about. I know that is easier said than done most days. Believe me, I know. But just let it sink in for a moment. Think of the one celebrity that you would give anything to meet. Yeh, you're even bigger, more famous than that to God. You really are. You should not have to perform for anyone. God loves you just the way you are and cries when you cry and applauds at your very existence. Why? Because He made you. He loves you. Period.

I may not know you, but hopefully, you have gotten to know me a little throughout this book. I am imperfect but perfectly loved. I have failed, but I am flawless. I have struggled, but I have superseded my own expectations. I have experienced loss, but I have been lavishly restored. I was broken, but now I am balanced. I was hurt, but now I am healed. I have been judged, but He made me justified. I was kicked when I was down, but I was kept by His hand from death and destruction. When I could not trust my own mind and thoughts, He held my hand and walked me through hell. There were times I was harsh as a result of the trauma in my life, but God's grace gave my mistakes meaning. There are no throw-away moments in life. I do not know how much plainer I can make any of this. You are loved. You are wanted. You are validated. You are everything. Feel it. Believe it. Receive it.

Whether you are a Christian or not really does not matter to me. I pray that Jesus reveals Himself to you and you receive Him. But that is between you and Him. All I can do is show you the love of God through me. Because you matter to me. You matter to God. Nothing in this life is wasted. Do not allow the enemy to beat you. You are bigger than that. You are stronger than that. In the words of TV evangelist James Robison:

"In this world, there is an enemy. In this world, there is a fight. Giving up... giving in to the enemy... is a fail."

You are not a failure. And failure cannot overtake your destiny. I don't know what you have been through. I don't know what lies the enemy has had you believing. But I would not feel this book is complete without offering you an invitation to know the Christ and be in a relationship with the Christ that I know, the Christ that loves me, the Christ that loves you, the Christ who brought me through life. The Christian life is not one without struggles. It is not one without pain. It is not one without loss. But it is one of love, hope, grace, forgiveness, healing, encouragement, and so many other wonderful things. You just have to remove the veil from your eyes and allow your pain to collide with the love of Christ. If you have never given your heart, your life, to the Lord, all it takes is you saying these simple words:

Father God, I humbly come before you. I confess with my mouth that I believe Jesus Christ is the Son of God, that He died on a cross to rescue me from sin and death and to restore me to the Father. I believe that Jesus rose from the grave. Please cleanse me of all unrighteousness. I receive Your forgiveness and ask that You take Your rightful place in my life as Lord and Savior. I choose You. I give myself to You. Come into my life and fill me with the Holy Spirit. Create in me a new heart. Help me to become a person who is truly loving… just like You. Heal me. Live in me. Restore me. Live through me. I need you. Thank You, Lord, that I am a new creation in Jesus Christ. I thank you that I am now Your child and as such entitled to all of the blessings and benefits that accompany salvation. I am Yours. In Jesus' mighty name, amen.

Over the years, I have heard multiple differing versions of the prayer above, and this is just a compilation of them. You can just say what you feel in your heart if that is more comfortable for you. I never try to force my faith on anyone. I almost grieve when I think where I might be today if it weren't for God. What you struggle with is not who you are. And you don't have to clean yourself up to come to God. He meets you where you are. Your greatest limitations are God's greatest opportunities to show Himself through you.

After David and I went through our divorce, the first post-divorce summer came upon us. Instead of the one month with dad, which we thought would not be good for Sofia and Lily, we decided to let each parent have the girls for every other week. When the first week came for the girls to be with David, it was very hard on me. But one sweet little gesture, one small step of love from Lily, made things so much better. After she was packed and ready to go to her dad's, she came to see me. Lily had in her hand Luke. Luke is one of her beloved stuffed teddy bears. She handed me Luke. I asked her why she was bringing Luke to me. Lily's reply was precious and priceless, "I know that sissy and I are going to be gone for a week. I didn't want you to get lonely, so I am giving Luke to you." I teared up and just gave her a big ole hug. A simple gesture with a big impact. It made all the difference in the world. I still missed Sofia and Lily, but Luke reminded me of their love for me. I still keep Luke in my room to this day.

One small step, one small gesture, one small word, one small choice, can change your life or someone else's life. I regrettably do not remember who said this, but it is worth sharing, *"The emotion that can break your heart is sometimes the very one that heals it."* Love has broken my heart more than once. But love is also what healed my heart. Again, I repeat, God has never failed me.

When I was reading through my journals, I found something that I had actually forgotten about. It is a good thing that I journal. On November 3, 2018, I wrote down something that God had said to me:

"Just as something has to BREAK in a woman—her water—before she can give birth, something had to BREAK in you in order for birthing to start."

"Birth" or "birthing" represents something new…new life. I went through much "breaking," but it had to happen in order for me to get to where I am today. Some old mindsets had to be broken. Some unhealthy relationships had to be broken. Pride had to be broken. Fear had to be broken. Unforgiveness had to be broken. The act of trying to do things on my own had to be broken. Lies in my head had to be broken. Pain had to be broken. Because in the breaking, a new life began. No excuses. No regrets. New hope. New life. Now, it is your turn. You have a lion in your wounds. Don't be silenced. It is your time to roar in victory.

"My Jesus"

-By: Anne Wilson

"Forever Reign"

-By: Hillsong Worship

"Speak The Name"

-By: Koryn Hawthorne featuring Natalie Grant

"You Say"

-By: Lauren Daigle

"What Mercy Did For Me"

-By: Micah Tyler, Crystal Yates, Joshua Sherman

"Be Alright"

-By: Evan Craft, Danny Gokey, Redimi2

"Known"

-By: Tauren Wells

"The Father's House"

-By: Cory Asbury

"Chainbreaker"

-By: Zach Williams

Chapter 27

Dancing With Destiny
Stories Of Hope

I am part of an online social media group. Who isn't, right? Well, one of the members of this particular group asked an interesting question one day. The question was, "If you could describe your current state in life with one sentence, what would it be?" I did not even hesitate because what immediately popped into my mind was, "Dancing with destiny." Then I paused for a moment and smiled. Why? Because that is truly how I feel. And I did not even realize it until that moment. What a beautiful, peaceful, exciting place to be in life. And that is my life. It just took many hills and valleys, twists and turns, laughter and tears, growth and gratitude to get here. But I am here, and that is all that matters.

Destiny is not a place, though. For me, destiny is a mindset. A perspective. A knowing. An expectation. Why? Well, destiny is about the future, even if it is two minutes from now. Destiny has absolutely nothing to do with the past. I do my best to live in the moment in order to make sure I do not miss anything of great importance because each minute of life is a gift. But as I sit here, I smile. Why? Because my past does not define me. The trauma I have experienced throughout life does not define me. Diagnosis or loss does not define me. God defines me. And He thinks I am amazing. And the thing about destiny, it hasn't happened yet. Every single thing that I have experienced in life, the good and the bad, has shaped me into the person I am today. I have a part in deciding what my tomorrow will be like, and I get to choose what kind of person I will be. That power is in my hands. And I choose to be loving, happy, thankful, giving, glowing, and so many more wonderful characteristics. I see my life as a million vibrant threads of silk being woven into a magnificent tapestry. And every single day, I have the honor of dancing through the threads and creating beauty with my life. Dance. Dream. Live.

One of the most valuable pieces of advice in my life came to me several years ago from none other than my daughter Sofia. Sofia was 11 years old at the time. My entire family was congregating in the kitchen. The kitchen is a favorite hang-out. It was the end of a long day. I normally try to be upbeat and positive, but it had just been one of those days that I felt "whooped." I was complaining... I mean, I was expressing various views on some current issues in life.

Okay, I was complaining, I admit it. In my defense, Psalm 142:2 does make this statement, *"I pour out my complaints before Him and tell Him all my troubles."* (NLT)

Moving on; it had just been one of those days where I felt like everything just went wrong, and the weight of the world was on my shoulders. I was exhausted, stressed, and just needed to breathe. I paused for a moment from sharing my feelings, and at that point, Sofia, who I thought had not even been listening, put down her phone, looked over at me, looked straight in my eyes, and said these words, "Mom, sometimes you just gotta get savage!" Sofia then turned away and went back to scrolling on her phone. I probably had that "deer in the headlights" look on my face. I had no idea what this statement meant in pre-teen language. But it silenced me. Being a bit of a "word nerd," I had to investigate all the meanings of the word "savage." I wanted to see if any of the meanings applied to me and the situation I found myself in. I looked into various definitions of the word savage and it has several meanings, but one implication of the word means to not be under the control of humans. I got it! And Sofia is a genius! I had been allowing people and issues get to me. I did not want to be led around or be controlled like that. So, I snapped out of it. To this day, the word "savage" has deep meaning to me. It reminds me not to let the things of this world turn my world upside down. So always remember, on those days when you feel like you are at your wits' end, in the words of a wise 11-year-old, "Sometimes you just gotta get savage!"

"Don't put your expectations in man. Put your expectations in God."

--To me, From God

I believe I have mentioned that I like going to the gym. When Covid hit, I dropped my gym membership and started working out at home. I miss working out at a gym, though, and need to re-join. The scales in my bathroom only confirm that need in my life. But prior to Covid, back in 2018, I was at the gym, and I just could not get through my workout. It was an odd feeling that I had never experienced. It was like a force was working against me. I had no strength. Keep in mind this would have been the year prior to David and me divorcing, and we were both just treading water in so many areas of our lives. Due to my lack of stamina, I gave up. I was not able to continue. I decided to go to the sauna and sit for a while. A bit perplexed at my situation, I asked God, "What's wrong with me?" I felt like God replied, "What's going on in the spiritual world is going on in the natural world as well. You are spiritually weak right now (from all that was going on in my life), so you are, in turn, physically weak right now."

I had never really thought about that scenario, but it made total sense. I had been reading my Bible, my devotional, and praying and fasting as I normally did. But my past and the struggles in my marriage had taken their toll on me. The only reason I even share this particular story is to let you know that you can be doing everything "right" but still end up depleted. I had felt like my prayers were not being answered, but I continued to pray. I had felt like my life was falling apart, but I still got up and out of bed each day. I had been feeling like a failure, but I knew God was still with me. My body was weak because my spirit was weak. At times like that, all you can do is trust God. I did. And my strength returned.

There was another time, several years back in 2017, that I had been really struggling with some circumstances that I was going through. I had experienced freedom in certain areas of my life, but I was still dealing with a bit of depression. I remember praying to God one day and sharing my heart with Him. I began with prayers of thanksgiving for all that God had done in my life up until that point. At the same time, there was a slight tinge of heaviness on me. I expressed to God, "So we have walked this journey, and after so many years, I finally feel free from my past (which I was not at all free in 2017), but those things that happened to me stole my joy, and I don't feel like my joy has been restored to me and I want my joy back." God, in His all-consuming love and tenderness, shed some light on something for me. Simply put, God told me, "Your joy was never stolen from you. Your joy cannot be taken from you. Your joy comes from Me, and I never left you. You allowed the things of this world to overshadow the joy I have placed in you. You do not get joy from the things or the people of this world. You get joy from Me." This was a simple but eye-opening truth that I needed to hear. I hope in some way it speaks to you as well with whatever circumstance you are faced with.

I assume if you have children or if you are involved in sports, you have probably heard the word "do-over." I remember playing with Sofia and Lily when they were little and if they messed up on something they would proclaim that it's a do-over…meaning they would get the opportunity to try again. Life is like that. If you "mess up", falter, didn't live up to yours or someone else's expectations, if you got lost somewhere along the road of life…you get a do-over. A do-over is an open door for a fresh start, a second chance at life, an opportunity to redo life. Think about that. It is an amazingly powerful thought. Not only powerful but full of hope. We all make mistakes, but our mistakes of the past do not determine our life in the future. Sometimes there are consequences to our mistakes. There are times we must make things right. We may have to ask for forgiveness. But the end result can be beautiful if you look at it from the right perspective: your life is a do-over. That is a gift. With God, each day in life is a new opportunity. Please do not waste it. You get to choose what kind of person you want to be and what direction your life will take. Please do not let the pain, regrets, or bitterness of the past wreak havoc on your future.

In the book of 1 Samuel in the Bible, we read the story of the first part of King David's life. As the story picks up in 1 Samuel 16, Samuel was one of Israel's greatest prophets. God told Samuel to anoint David, a young shepherd boy, the youngest of eight brothers, as the next king of Israel. This was without a doubt perplexing to all since King Saul was still alive and on the throne. On top of that, David was the youngest of eight brothers, and his life was viewed as the most insignificant. My point in all of this is that David's brothers saw a shepherd. God saw a king. David did not even know that he was a king, but his faith in God led him to be a king. You may not even see your own greatness, but God does. And today is the first day of the rest of your life. If your life is at an intersection of a do-over, make the choices that are going to make your life beautiful. What if something that you have seen as an interruption in your life has actually been an intervention of God? Think about that. What you have seen as a setback in life may have just been a setup by God.

"…for everything serves Your plans."

--Psalm 119:91 (NLT)

I am a huge believer in setting goals as well as writing down dreams and visions that I have for the future. I am someone who needs something to work towards. It keeps me focused. Recently Sofia, Lily, and I made vision boards. Once the three of us cut out pictures from magazines of things that we desire for our lives, we all pasted our pictures onto thick posterboard. The girls had everything from dogs, college, houses, vehicles, sports, good grades, swimming pool, and marriage, to name a few items for their boards. I then chatted with Sofia and Lily and asked them what they could each do to work towards their dreams and goals. A few noted responses were: pray, study more, practice (sports) and get good jobs. At this point, I drew a diagram featuring their responses. We decided that studying harder would lead to better grades. Better grades would lead to better choices of colleges. Being serious in college could lead to better job opportunities. A good job could lead to the finances to buy some of the things they desired. We discussed that it was important to keep God in the center of everything. My final point to Sofia and Lily was that achieving their goals would all begin with effort. They understood. The same holds true in life in general. If you want your life to be better, if you want to experience healing and wholeness, if you need new friends in your life, if you desire change in any way, it begins with you. You must put forth the effort.

In February of 2017, I was praying one morning and listening to calming, meditation music. Suddenly I heard God ask me, "What would a perfect world look like to you?" I thought for a moment and answered, "No sorrow, no pain, perfect love, no condemnation...." My list went on. Then I heard again, "Then strive for these things." I knew immediately what God meant. We all must put forth effort and do our part. If you want peace in your life, extend peace to others. If you want love in your life, get rid of the garbage from your past, trust, give love and receive love. If you want emotionally healthy people in your life, then get yourself emotionally healthy. If you don't want to be judged, then don't be judgmental towards others. If you want romance in your life, be romantic. I could go on and on, but the simple meaning is this: Put out in the world what you want to receive from the world. Do your part.

Get a vision in your heart and mind of what you desire in life, then work towards what is in your heart. In doing so, also realize that you must put some work into the desired results. God isn't going to just drop everything you want into your life. And every single thing you seek may not come to pass. Sometimes this is because God knows that some things you want in life might not be the best for you. At the same time, you need to be realistic with your dreams. I would be ecstatic if I could sing like Celine Dion. But I am wise enough to know that God did not bless me with an amazing voice, and I was not put on this earth to be a professional singer. Trust me, if you heard me belt out a tune, you would agree. But you do have something that is explicitly you. If you don't know what it is, ask friends and family what you are good at.

I love this quote by Albert Einstein, *"Everyone is a genius, but if you judge a fish by its ability to climb a tree, it will live its whole life believing it is stupid."* Einstein believed intelligence is a choice. His message here is that you should not let a false belief take root in your mind by what others say about you or judge you by. The bottom line is that a fish was not created to climb a tree, but a fish is exceptional at swimming. I think you get the point. Your choices, your future, your life is in your hands. God will walk every step with you, and I pray that you seek Him for wisdom and guidance. Maybe it's time to take that first step. My life is a do-over. I intend to expend every ounce of energy, love, wisdom, and effort towards achieving my goals and making life beautiful for others and for myself. I believe that is God's dream for us.

"What a wonderful thought it is that some of the best days of our lives haven't even happened yet."

--Anne Frank

The main reason I shared these last few stories is that I would like to shower you with hope and encouragement. My life has not been perfect…far from it…and that's alright. God does not expect perfection from me. People have let me down or hurt me. God is bigger than the circumstances in my life. I have made bad decisions in my life. God was with me as I walked through the consequences of my bad decisions. My brokenness led me to believe that I wasn't worthy of love or being treated respectfully. God exposed those lies of the enemy. My emotional wellness was shattered. God has revealed to me, along with the help of an exceptional therapist, how to take my thoughts captive, find the root of the distress, and learn to walk through what I am experiencing and live again. Live life. That's what I want for you. That's what God wants for you. The pain you have experienced in life is no match for the passionate love that God has for you. He wants you to see what is already there and that your life, your potential, your very being, is worth fighting for. In the words of one of my favorite authors:

"God's love for us isn't threatened by our broken pieces. We are each a work in progress, and he's the one completing the work, with all kinds of love and patience."

--Shauna Niequist, from the devotional, "Savor: Living Abundantly Where You Are, As You Are"

Everything God creates is a masterpiece. You are a work of art. God molded you and shaped you. He formed you in your mother's womb. God instilled in you all that you require to do this thing called life. Each day is a new day, a new opportunity to dance. As I personally curtsy, twirl, and flow with the music of life, I smile as I sashay myself through the illuminating colors of vibrant threads that are establishing my life. My wish for you is that you do the same. Take God's hand. Let Him lead. And dance your way into healing, wholeness, life, love, and the destiny that was always meant for you. I leave you with these songs of hope and love:

"Champion"

-By: Bethel Music with Dante Bowe

"Until Grace"

-By: Tauren Well and Gary LeVox of Rascal Flatts

"The Blessing"

-By: Cody Carnes, Kari Jobe, and Elevation Worship

Chapter 28

It's A Wrap

Every person's journey is different. Every person's struggles are different. Every person's life is different. This has been the story of my life. But my story is still being written. I wanted to share my trials and challenges with you. I sought to reveal to you what trauma can look like and the damage it can cause in life. I aspired to unveil how forgiveness towards myself and towards others, as well as therapy and God, completely turned my life around. My deepest desire is to demonstrate that there is hope, regardless of what you have been through. In life, you win or learn. You never lose.

I must point out; I am not a doctor. I am not a therapist. I am not a minister. I am just me. And I am happy to just be me. My greatest wish would be that my story can inspire you, make you think, and give you encouragement and a resolve to be the best you that you can be. If there is one song that sums my life up better than any other, it would be:

"Look What You've Done"

-By: Tasha Layton

Throughout this book, I mentioned many different people that I have met over the years and how their insights spoke to me. Although I included quotes by them, these people may not share my same ideas, views, or opinions. These people positively impacted my life, so I wanted to bring you their words of wisdom to shine a little light into your life.

Pain and passion. Trauma and love. Hills and valleys. Beauty from ashes. Healing. Strength. Hope. I sincerely pray that today you choose to move forward. I have such joy within me. And my past is just that, the past. It has no hold on me. I have such great peace within me, and I choose to live in the moment for all life has to offer. I have such great expectations for the future, and I realize just how much responsibility for that future is in my hands. I have such great faith in my God, in Whom all of this is possible. I thank God for unveiling truth to me. Because it was when my pain collided with His passion that my healing began. You were never meant to merely exist. There is a purpose for your life. Take hold of life and live.

I must share three more songs with you that breathe life into my soul. I also want to leave you with more inspirational quotes and one more scripture that sums it up for me. I hope these words speak to your heart in the same way they speak to mine. May the lies the enemy has spoken to you be unveiled, and you see truth. The truth that you are loved. Prayers and hugs to you. You got this.

"Mercy"
-By: Elevation Worship and Maverick City Music

"Move Your Heart"
-By: Maverick City Music and Upperroom

"Rattle"
-By: Elevation Worship

"If it's not good yet… then God is not done. The difficulty is not the end of our story."

--Louie Giglio, Leader of Passion City Church, Founder of the Passion Movement, Author and Speaker

"The deeper call for courage comes when you let go with nothing ahead to grab."

"Only in letting go are your hands free to grab on to the next thing."

"You can trust God when you don't see the future because He can."

--Annie Downs, Author and Speaker

"I am passionately in love with God because he listens to me.

He hears my prayers and answers them.

As long as I live I'll keep praying to him,

for he stoops down to listen to my heart's cry.

Death once stared me in the face,

and I was close to slipping into the dark shadows.

I was terrified and overcome with sorrow.

I cried out to the Lord, 'God come and save me!'

He was so kind, so gracious to me.

Because of his passion toward me,

he made everything right, and he restored me.

So I've learned from my experience

that God protects the vulnerable.

For I was broken and brought low,

but he answered me and came to my rescue!

Now I can say to myself and to all,

'Relax and rest, be confident and serene,

for the Lord rewards fully those who simply trust in him."

--Psalm 116: 1-7 (TPT)

"For you, Lord, have delivered me from death,

my eyes from tears,

my feet from stumbling,

that I may walk before the Lord

in the land of the living."

--Psalm 116: 8-9 (NIV)

Credits

Introduction:

1. *Merriam-Webster*, s.v. "unveiled" (v.), https://www.merriam-webster.com/dictionary/unveiled.

2. *Merriam-Webster,* s.v. "perspective" (n.), https://www.merriam-webster.com/dictionary/perspective.

Chapter 1:

1. Chad Veach, Kim Meeder: *Guests on "Life Today with James Robison."*

Chapter 2:

1. *#Not Anymore*, https://civilrights.missouri.edu. Sexual Violence Prevention for Students.

Chapter 3:

1. Shauna Niequist, *Savor: Living Abundantly Where You Are, As You Are* (Michigan: Zondervan, 2015), 308.

2. https://www.brainyquotes.com/quotes/khalil_gibran_386848.

3. Joni Eareckson Tada, Toni Collier, Ally and Josh Taylor: Guests on *"Life Today with James Robison."*

Chapter 4:

1. Zig Ziglar, *Better Than Good* (Tennessee: Integrity Publishers, 2006).

2. https://insight.org/resources/daily-devotional/individual/the-broken-wing2.

3. https://seancroxton.com/quote-of-the-day/048.

4. Max Lucado, Erwin McManus: Guests on *"Life Today with James Robison."*

Chapter 5:

1. Joyce Meyer: Guest on *"Life Today with James Robison."*

Chapter 12:

1. Shauna Niequist, *Savor: Living Abundantly Where You Are, As You Are* (Michigan: Zondervan, 2015), 132.

Chapter 16:

1. Michael Brown, Elizabeth Hasselbeck: Guests on *"Life Today with James Robison."*

Chapter 17:

1. https://psycom.net.
https://EMDR.com.

Chapter 18:

1. Erwin Raphael McManus, *The Way Of The Warrior* (New York: WaterBrook, 2019), xiv.

2. https://americanart.si.edu. George Santayana, *The Life of Reason*, 1905. From the series *Great Ideas of Western Man*.

3. Ruth Soukup, *Do It Scared* (Zondervan, 2019).

4. https://fdrlibrary.org/eleanor-roosevelt.

Chapter 21:

1. *Graves Into Gardens,* Elevation Worship, Brandon Lake. Bethel Music Publishing, Maverick City Publishing Worldwide, Brandon Lake Music. 2020.

2. Kim Meeder, Todd Lollar, Toni Collier, Lecrea: Guests on *"Life Today with James Robison."*

Chapter 22:

1. Shauna Niequist, *Savor: Living Abundantly Where You Are, As You Are* (Michigan: Zondervan, 2015), 254.

2. https://www.brainyquote.com/quotes/terrell_owens_429919.

3. Ben Courson, Andrew Brunson: Guests on *"Life Today with James Robison."*

4. *Life Application Study Bible*, New Living Translation, Second Edition (Illinois: Tyndale House Publishers, Inc., 1996).

Chapter 23:

1. Annie Downs, *100 Days to Brave* (Michigan: Zondervan, 2017).

2. Michele Cushatt, *I Am* (Michigan, Zondervan, 2017), 274.

3. Tony Evans, Bobby Petrocelli: Guests on *"Life Today with James Robison."*

Chapter 27:

1. *Merriam-Webster*, s.v. "savage (v)" https://merriam-webster.com/dictionary/savage.

2. https://quotefancy.com/quote/766669/Anne-Frank-What-a-wonderful-thought-it-is-that-some-of-the-best-days-of-our-lives-haven-t

3. Shauna Niequist, *Savor: Living Abundantly Where You Are, As You Are* (Michigan, Zondervan, 2015), 219.

Chapter 28:

1. Annie Downs, *100 Days to Brave* (Michigan, Zondervan, 2017), 131-132.